LIFE IN THE
TIME OF OIL

LIFE IN THE TIME OF OIL

A Pipeline and Poverty in Chad

LORI LEONARD

INDIANA UNIVERSITY PRESS
Bloomington & Indianapolis

This book is a publication of

Indiana University Press
Office of Scholarly Publishing
Herman B Wells Library 350
1320 East 10th Street
Bloomington, Indiana 47405 USA

iupress.indiana.edu

The paper used in this publication meets the minimum requirements
of the American National Standard for Information Sciences—Permanence
of Paper for Printed Library Materials, ANSI Z39.48-1992.

Manufactured in the United States of America

Cataloging information is available from the Library of Congress.

ISBN 978-0-253-01980-6 (cloth)
ISBN 978-0-253-01983-7 (paperback)
ISBN 978-0-253-01987-5 (ebook)

1   2   3   4   5   21   20   19   18   17   16

For Loïc and Ulrich, *les étoiles brillantes*

CONTENTS

ACKNOWLEDGMENTS

This book was a very long time in the making, and I have incurred many debts along the way.

The extensive fieldwork that went into this book would not have been possible without the support of the National Science Foundation and its Human and Social Dynamics Program (BCS-0527280). Support for the project was also provided by the Law and Social Sciences program at the NSF (SES-0721712), the New Century Scholars program of the J. William Fulbright Foundation, the Health, Environment, and Economic Development (HEED) program of the Fogarty International Center at the National Institutes of Health (R21 TW006518-01), the Population Center and the Center for a Livable Future at Johns Hopkins University, and the Woodrow Wilson International Center for Scholars (WWICS), where I began writing this book during a yearlong residential fellowship in an environment that was nothing short of a dream. I am grateful to these institutions for their support and especially for their recognition of the value of extended ethnographic fieldwork. I am also grateful to the people within these institutions who I know— or at least suspect—championed this project. They include Thomas Baerwald at the NSF, Rachel Nugent at the NIH, Andy Cherlin at the Hopkins Population Center, and Steve McDonald and Michael Van Dusen at the WWICS.

The chapters in this book have benefited from the feedback of careful readers and generous critics. My thanks go especially to Omolade Adunbi and Daniel Jordan Smith, who reviewed the book manuscript for Indiana University Press, and to the members of the Africa Seminar at Johns Hopkins—a remarkable Friday afternoon gathering organized by Sara Berry and Pier Larson that is a model for what an academic seminar should be. Some of the regulars at the seminar who saw early drafts of these chapters and pushed me to reshape them include Sara Berry, Thomas Cousins, Julia Cummiskey, Joshua Garoon, Siba Grovogui, Anatoli Ignatov, Jacqui Ignatova, Isaac Kamola, Pier Larson, Kirsten Moore-Sheeley, Randy Packard, Lindsey Reynolds, and Alice Wiemers. I also presented early versions of chapters at the Population Studies and Training Center seminar at Brown University, where the comments of Saida Hodzic, now a colleague at Cornell, Daniel Jordan Smith, and Nick Townsend were particularly helpful, and at seminars organized by the Institute for African Development at Cornell

University, the Institute for African Studies at Emory University, and the African Studies Program at Indiana University, which were occasions to receive helpful feedback from Africanists and to meet Dee Mortensen, my editor at IUP, who has been supportive from the start. I am grateful to Muna Ndulo at Cornell, Clifford Crais at Emory, and Maria Grosz-Ngaté at Indiana for those invitations. Presentations at the Mailman School of Public Health at Columbia University and the Jiann-Ping Hsu College of Public Health at Georgia Southern University, and the interventions of J. Paul Martin, Alison Scott, and their students, sharpened my thinking about the health and human rights dimensions of the project.

I was at John Hopkins University while doing the fieldwork for this project, and I am indebted to colleagues and students at Hopkins whose work and support for this project helped to shape it in big and small ways. Early on I worked with Veena Das, Ranendra Kumar Das, and Todd Meyers in the Department of Anthropology on a comparative project that helped solidify the methods I used in conducting household surveys, which were an important starting point for the fieldwork I eventually undertook. A number of students accompanied me to the field or worked on the project from Baltimore, including Sima Berendes, Claire Breedlove, Joshua Garoon, Maura Lillis, Leah Maniero, Lindsey Reynolds, Beth Rubenstein, and Jamie Saltsman, as well as Stephen Wissow from Reed College. The brightest light in my time at Hopkins was an extraordinary cohort of doctoral students who lived through "the Chad project" and whose creativity, care, and friendship prolonged my stay at Hopkins and made it a productive place to be. They include Alison Scott, Joshua Garoon, Emma Tsui, Kate Muessig, Will Dyckman, Lindsey Reynolds, Stephanie Farquhar, Morgan Philbin, and Amelia Buttress.

This project had several rocky starts in Chad that taught me firsthand about oil rents, the Chadian legal system, and the high-stakes business of doing research on a model pipeline project. I am grateful to Daugla Doumagoum Moto and the Centre de Support en Santé International in N'Djamena for providing me with a stable operating base and an institutional home for the project in Chad. Many people assisted with fieldwork over the years; I am especially grateful to Gerard, Ali, Appolinaire, Nangbe, Hippolyte, Oundade, Jeremie, Ngarmane, and Patcha. Ngondoloum Salathiel belongs in a category all by himself; it is not hyperbole to say that this project would not have been possible without him. A son of canton Miandoum and the village of Ngalaba, he was my constant companion and the person who held things together even when I was around.

I owe much to the families in canton Miandoum who were part of this project. They were generous with humor, hospitality, information, and time despite their struggles and disappointments. Only a fraction of our exchanges made their way onto these pages, but the many hours spent in their villages and concessions was vital to understanding the project and what it meant to them and to others living in its shadow.

I am fortunate to have a dense social network in Chad that preceded this project and was strengthened by it. Spending time in Chad was a treat because of Moussa and Esther and their family, who opened their house in N'Djamena to me and whose friendship now spans half my lifetime. The extended Massingar family holds a special place in my heart and will always make Chad feel like home. Yaya Monique, Rosalie, Patricia, Nestoran, Jonathan, Essaie, Gerard, Paul, Pierre, Getty, Benjamin, and especially Franck, Tatiana, Loic, and Ulrich will always be family to me. My friends at the Prestige and Tchad Evasion, as well as Adoum, Freddy, Mahamat, Yacoub, Zenaba, and so many others, have been kind and generous in ways I can never hope to repay.

My parents asked often and anxiously after this book, probably wishing that my extended trips to Chad and my absences during the holidays would come to an end, though never saying so. My father's love of language and stories and his writerly sensibilities and my mother's sharply analytic mind and her unflinching realism about the world and pragmatic attitude about finding what needs to be done to make it better have given me both inspiration and lots of room to wander. And finally there is Siba, who, somewhat unbelievably, gave up summers in southern France to accompany me to the oil fields of Chad. I don't know anyone else who could have reconfigured his life in such a way or—more important—anyone else who would have. I hope he sees his fingerprints all over these pages.

LIFE IN THE TIME OF OIL

ONE

An Experiment in Development

> The entire country has its eyes turned to the Doba region, which has
> become the center of national attention with the activities of CONOCO.
> Of course, finding oil is always a roll of the dice. But when the work of
> this company is crowned with success, supporting industries and complex
> and specialized installations will proliferate. The key to the problem of
> development will be found, and we will be able to make over the entirety
> of Chad.
>   —President François Ngarta Tombalbaye, *Info-Tchad*,
>   December 19, 1973

On my first trip to canton Miandoum, just as the Chad-Cameroon Petroleum
Development and Pipeline Project was getting underway, Firmin took me to see
le premier puits—the first well.[1] It stood in a clearing on an abandoned plot of land,
surrounded by scrub brush and high grasses, and was bright red, the color of a fire
hydrant. A small metal plaque commemorating the oil find was affixed to the
well. By the time I made the pilgrimage to the well with Firmin, everyone knew
that other wells—hundreds of them—would follow. Firmin wanted to be photo-
graphed next to the first well. The photographs I took of him remind me of others
I took of people posing with their prized possessions—not oil wells, but radios,
bicycles, mobile phones, or decorative pots and pans. Firmin was wearing a Chicago
Bulls jersey. He had one of his hands on the well and was leaning into it, possessively.
His other hand grasped the handle of the hoe that was perched on his shoulder. In
those images he seems to embody the tensions and transformations, the hopes and
dreams of a nation on the verge of something big. The photographs capture an
instant of wide openness, a moment of promise when it seemed possible that
Tombalbaye's dream might finally come true.

Nowhere in Chad was the connection between oil and development more
deeply engrained than in canton Miandoum, where Conoco conducted explor-
atory drilling in the 1970s. The year after Tombalbaye announced that prospecting
operations were underway in the Doba basin, euphoric headlines appeared in the
national newspaper, the *Canard Déchaîné*. Conoco had struck oil! The year after
that, the president was assassinated in a military coup.[2] In the decades that followed, Firmin's parents and their families, friends, and neighbors took care of

Conoco's successful test well, organizing work parties to clear brush from the site. A generation of children grew up participating in these work parties, or minding their younger brothers and sisters while their parents worked. They remember the open sludge pit next to the well that Western Drilling covered over—though not until 1992. They remember their parents' warnings to stay away from the pit, and how their oxen occasionally fell into it and drowned or had to be pulled out with ropes and were useless after that because they were too weak to do any work. They remember how people said the well would be their "future wealth."

On October 18, 2000, more than a quarter of a century after Tombalbaye set Chad's oil-producing ambitions in motion and just a few months before I took the photographs of Firmin at the first well, government officials, executives of ExxonMobil, and representatives of the World Bank gathered in Komé, a village about ten kilometers to the west of the well site, for the groundbreaking ceremony that marked the beginning of construction on the pipeline project. The project that was about to get underway would be carried out as a joint venture between a consortium of global oil companies, including ExxonMobil, Chevron, and Petronas, the World Bank, and the governments of Chad and Cameroon. It would be one of the largest private sector investments on the African continent, and would cost more than $4 billion. Investors expected that over the next twenty-five to thirty years the project would produce one billion barrels of oil from three separate oil fields in Chad's Doba basin, including the Miandoum oil field where Conoco had drilled the first well. The oil would be transported more than one thousand kilometers through an underground pipeline across Cameroon to oil tankers moored off the port of Kribi in the Atlantic Ocean. Its sale in global markets was expected to generate more than $2 billion in revenues for Chad.

Residents of the oil field region sat under the blistering sun outside the gates of the consortium's base camp to watch the event on a giant screen suspended from a construction crane. One by one the dignitaries assembled there rose to make speeches about how oil could reduce poverty and lead to development—not just in Chad but across the African continent. According to the speakers, poverty reduction did not hinge on the proliferation of the industries and infrastructure Tombalbaye had envisioned but instead on Africa's ability to attract more private capital and investment. The project these dignitaries were in Komé to inaugurate was a model—a prototype—for how to do this.[3] This approach to poverty reduction required governments to partner with multinational oil companies and global financial institutions and undertake internal reforms to become more transparent, accountable, and fiscally responsible. Callisto Madavo, the World Bank's vice president for the Africa region, reminded those gathered for the occasion that the project in Chad was a test case for this model of development that would reverberate far beyond the oil field region and Chad:

Together, we need to demonstrate that petroleum resources can be used to lift our people out of deep poverty, while protecting the environment and respecting the rights of communities and individuals. Together, we can encourage other private investors to consider projects in Africa which will bring them good returns but also—with imaginative public policy and good government—improve African society at large. And, together, we can show how a partnership between governments, multinational companies, multilateral financial institutions, and local communities can benefit everyone. The world is watching this experiment closely and we should take advantage of that attention.

Less than eight years later, on September 9, 2008, the World Bank announced that the experiment the world was watching had come to an untimely end. The bank's announcement that it was withdrawing from the project came even as the pace of oil production in the Doba basin was accelerating and as the consortium was expanding the project to bring new oil fields and hundreds of additional oil wells online. The announcement took the form of a press release the World Bank posted to its website. It contained just 328 words. According to the World Bank, the government had failed to invest its oil revenues according to the prescribed poverty-reducing formula. The day after the announcement, the *New York Times* published an obituary for the project. "One of the most ambitious efforts to escape Africa's resource curse," wrote the *Times* correspondent, "ended quietly this week" (Polgreen 2008).

Life in the Time of Oil is a story of one of the grandest experiments in development of the late neoliberal era, and of an oil pipeline in Chad that was supposed to reduce poverty. I became interested in oil and in the space that it occupied in the social imaginary and in daily life in Chad long before the pipeline project was conceived. When I lived in Chad in the late 1980s and again in the early 1990s, oil was present even in its absence. ExxonMobil, which operated in Chad as Esso, had been exploring for oil in Chad since 1977, several years after Conoco's initial find. Drilling companies like Parker and Western and the Texas oil men that worked for them came and went. Their movements were the subject of constant speculation. Were oil prices too low for them to make a profit? Was there not enough oil in the ground after all? Did their departure mean that political trouble was afoot? Were they back for good this time? In Chad, development dreams have always hinged on oil. For more than a quarter of a century people anticipated oil and talked about it. Oil was something out there on the horizon, a harbinger of hope and the promise of a future that would be different.

Many of the dreams people had were fantastic, as oil dreams are. They were also fantastically imprecise and malleable, and their tenor and content shifted over time. What, exactly, would oil do? Tombalbaye saw oil as the catalyst for industrialization. His was the dream of the developmental state. In contrast, the World Bank saw oil as Chad's key to global markets, as the force that would attract more private investment in the country and supply the resources for poverty reduction. This was the neoliberal dream. The juxtaposition of these dreams illustrates just how fungible oil can be. It has the capacity to animate different types of development projects, to span development paradigms, and to slip into new discourses about development and poverty reduction. The notion that oil was a "strategic prize" (Yergin 1993)—a constant in these visions and in people's everyday conversations about oil—was especially intriguing given the "curse" the *New York Times* correspondent referenced and the fact that oil has been a bane for the continent more often than it has been a boon.

While many African states are now oil producers, the Chad-Cameroon Petroleum Development and Pipeline Project was also particularly fascinating and important to study because of how it was discursively positioned as a template for all other extractive industry projects on the continent and beyond. The project was described as a model, a test case, and an experiment because it combined elements of the World Bank's Poverty Reduction and Good Governance agenda (Craig and Porter 2006) in unparalleled fashion. Development is a problematic concept, but because the pipeline project was the prototype for a new generation of efforts to reduce poverty even some who were skeptical about 'development' and oil as a medium for it expressed a wait-and-see attitude about the Chad project (Ferguson 2006; Guyer 2002). In some ways, a postconflict[4] country located thousands of kilometers from any seaport seemed an unlikely site for a model pipeline project. On the other hand, it was precisely those characteristics that made it possible for the World Bank to formulate such an ambitious experiment in the first place.

This book is an account of crucial dimensions of that experiment. It is the result of dozens of extended periods of research I conducted in Chad between 2000, when construction on the pipeline was just getting underway, and 2012, four years after the World Bank announced its withdrawal from the project. It analyzes the implementation of the pipeline project as a development model through the transformations it engendered in canton Miandoum, and a collection of villages in the canton that sit atop and around the edges of the Miandoum oil field. At the broadest level the kinds of questions I ask in this book are questions that critical scholars of development have long been asking: What was this model that the world was watching, and what did it do? What effects did this experiment in development produce, and were these the effects we anticipated?

A Model Pipeline

When people like the *New York Times* correspondent say the pipeline project in Chad was an effort "to escape Africa's resource curse," they typically mean that it was an effort to keep the government from looting or mismanaging oil revenues. The resource curse thesis refers to the paradox that countries with oil wealth experience slower rates of economic growth and have worse development outcomes than countries without these resources.[5] The thesis occupies a conspicuous place in the scholarship on oil and Africa, a continent where the extractive industries drive foreign direct investment (United Nations Conference on Trade and Development 2013). There are multiple theories about why African oil producers perform so poorly, all of which surfaced in the debates about the pipeline project, but the lack of "good governance" and the propensity of the state to plunder are core concerns of resource curse theorists. In Chad these narratives were taken up by civil society groups and activists who opposed the project and argued that oil would not reduce poverty because the government was corrupt and had a history of human rights violations and therefore could not be trusted to manage oil wealth in ways that would benefit the poor.

The preproject cautions of the activists and the postmortems—the bookends for the project—are striking not because of their convergence or the sense they convey that the activists were right all along but because the dynamics they describe were far more complicated than either of these accounts suggests. Michael Watts (2004a) has argued that one of the problems with the literature on the resource curse is that it ignores global oil companies and the forms of capitalism enclave extraction engenders. Global oil companies are at the center of my account, but the project in Chad was not a typical oil export project in that it was not strictly a joint venture between ExxonMobil, which represented the consortium in Chad, and the Chadian state. The World Bank also played a critical role in the project. The consortium invited the World Bank to participate as a way to mitigate its investment risks. The bank's involvement was also supposed to ease public concerns about the government's record of corruption and other abuses. By taking on the role of "moral guarantor" for the project, the bank was able to attract additional private investment in the project and acquire policy influence out of all proportion to its own financial stake in the venture (Darrow 2003).

The World Bank used that influence to assemble what it described as an "unprecedented framework" for poverty reduction (World Bank 2000). At its broadest, the framework involved integrating Chad into global markets through the sale of Chadian oil, reforming governance, and building institutional capacity in Chad to manage the emerging oil economy. The framework combined market integration with governance reforms—the two pillars of the World Bank's newest development paradigm, which retains the neoliberal emphasis on market liberalization and the promotion of private sector enterprise but pairs that agenda with institutionalism, and with the recognition of the importance of a "capable state" in dealing with, among other things, social instability caused by market reforms and austerity measures (Craig and Porter 2006).

At the level of implementation, the framework—the "Chad model," as it came to be known—was made up of multiple components. One of those components was a $24 million *Petroleum Sector Management Capacity Building Project* financed by the World Bank to promote the development of Chad's oil sector. The project was supposed to strengthen government capacity to manage the Doba basin project and promote additional private sector investment in Chad's oil industry. It called for the government to "create an environment favorable to private sector development" by revising laws and environmental regulations to make Chad more attractive to oil companies and by developing the technical capacities and infrastructure to manage geological, geophysical, and economic information to attract exploration beyond the Doba basin oil fields. The project also invested in training government officials in how to negotiate and manage contracts with potential investors.

Another component of the framework, and the one referenced in the World Bank's postmortem for the project, was the *Revenue Management Plan* that directed the government to use oil revenues from the Doba basin oil fields for poverty reduction. This plan, also known as Law 001, established a legal framework for the use of oil money. Ten percent of revenues from royalties and dividends were to be sequestered in an offshore account for "future generations." Of the remaining revenues from royalties and dividends, 80 percent, and eventually 95 percent, were to be spent in "priority" sectors of the economy including education, health, agriculture, infrastructure, and rural development.[6] Five percent were earmarked for poverty reduction projects in the oil-producing region. Government spending was supervised by the Collège de Contrôle et de Surveillance des Revenus Pétrolières (the CCSRP), a body with civil society representation that was supposed to follow the money. The CCSRP vetted proposals for poverty reduction spending from government ministries and authorized disbursements from the government's account.

A third component of the framework, and the one that implicated the consortium directly and that I examine most closely in this book, was a bundle of policies to mitigate the social and environmental impacts of the Doba basin project on local communities, including the villages in canton Miandoum. The policies were collected in a twenty-volume, 5,200-page *Environmental Management Plan* (*EMP*) that included environmental assessments, supporting documents, and a series of plans that were based on global standards and industry best practices, including plans for involuntary resettlement, waste management, oil spills, cultural property, and worker health and safety (Moynihan et al. 2004).[7] The plans were supposed to help people displaced by the project to rehabilitate themselves and to recover from the loss of their land and their livelihoods. The standards and risk mitigation policies are required elements of high-risk projects funded by the World Bank, and the EMP was vetted and approved by the bank as a condition of project financing.

Finally, the implementation of these project components was monitored by multiple monitoring bodies with overlapping mandates. The consortium had its own compliance monitoring team, and the World Bank financed the creation of two oversight bodies in Chad and two external monitoring bodies. In Chad, the CCSRP monitored the government's use of oil money and an inter-ministerial committee known as the Comité Technique National de Suivi et de Contrôle (CTNSC) monitored compliance with the EMP and oversaw the implementation of the *Petroleum Sector Capacity Management Project*. The International Finance Corporation (IFC) hired an External Compliance Monitoring Group (ECMG), which also monitored compliance with the EMP, and the World Bank Group's board appointed an International Advisory Group (IAG) to advise the World Bank President and the governments of Chad and Cameroon on project implementation and on the achievement of the project's poverty reduction goals. The IAG and the ECMG both traveled regularly to the oil field region and posted their observations and recommendations to public websites.

The World Bank's "unprecedented framework" worked to shape the behavior of individual farmers as well as relations between the government and private investors, the government and its citizens, global oil companies and farmers in the oil field region, and farmers and their families. In writing about the resource curse, journalists, activists, and the World Bank focused on one actor and one set of relations in isolation, obscuring the linkages between these multiple efforts to govern. Michel Foucault (1991) described the task of government as being the establishment of a link between individual conduct, the management of the family, and the running of the state that operates in both directions—upward and downward. The person who learns to self-govern can apply these principles to the management of her family and, in turn, to the running of the state, while the well-run state can, through policy, serve as a model for the management of the family and for individual behavior.

Of course, other linkages are possible and neither development models nor neoliberal processes are this coherent.[8] The project as it unfolded in Chad was not readily discernible from policy documents like the *Petroleum Sector Management Capacity Building Project*, the *Revenue Management Plan*, and the *Environmental Management Plan*. One of the problems with the writing on the project is that it relies overwhelmingly on the analysis of official policy documents, which lend the project far more coherence than it actually had. Scholars, journalists, and project monitors proceeded as if the project could be grasped by studying the political rationalities and associated technologies described in these policy documents and as if the project and its effects were almost as easily modified as the documents themselves. This writing sheds little light on the existing, unfolding project or how the model actually worked.

In the chapters that follow, I examine the model through the implementation of the social and environmental risk mitigation policies in the oil field region. What I am tracing in these ethnographies of policy are situated forms of corporate and transnational governance, but ones that had linkages and effects beyond the oil field region. The risk mitigation policies, like the other components of the model, were pedagogical tools, even if molding farmers and producing neoliberal subjects were not the consortium's primary preoccupations. Families in canton Miandoum were critical sites for instruction and training, and my fieldwork was oriented around particular families in the canton that I followed over the life of the project. From this vantage point I observed how global standards and model policies became entangled in social life and family relations, reconfiguring them in ways the policy documents failed to capture. The writing on the project and the resource curse obscured these intimate entanglements and their effects, which occurred in peripheral sites of extraction but shaped the outcome of the World Bank's model project and the macroeconomy of oil.

Policy in Action

The area known as the oil field region is in Chad's Doba basin, in the Logone Orientale, an administrative region in southwestern Chad that borders Cameroon to the west and the Central African Republic to the south. The consortium referred to the oil field region as the Oil Field Development Area, or OFDA. By the consortium's estimates, the OFDA covered roughly 100,000 hectares, or 400 square miles (EEPCI 2010). Most of the 1,070 kilometer pipeline is in Cameroon, but the oil fields and project infrastructure are in Chad, most of it in the rural cantons of Bero, Komé, and Miandoum. The original plans for the project included the development of 287 oil wells in three oil fields, the Bolobo, Komé, and Miandoum oil fields, that the consortium brought online in 2003 and 2004 (EEPCI 1999b, vol. 3, sec. 3.4). The consortium also built a network of dirt roads, an electrical grid with thousands of pylons to support high-voltage power lines, an airstrip, work camps, supply yards, and oil collection and pumping stations (Guyer 2002).

The project was not a classic case of enclave extraction of the kind described by James Ferguson (2005, 2006). While the consortium's base camps and storage yards were walled off from the surrounding communities and tightly secured, oil wells, roads, high-voltage power lines, borrow pits, and other aspects of project infrastructure were scattered throughout the oil field region. The consortium announced that few families would be displaced because it had designed the project around existing villages but that it would have to occupy thousands of hectares of agricultural land between these villages. Project roads wound around villages, and oil wells and electrical pylons sat in the middle of agricultural fields where people farmed. Residents crisscrossed project roads on the way to their fields or neighboring villages. They slept under the glare of stadium lights from the pumping and gathering station and grew accustomed to the around-the-clock whirring of machines at nearby drilling sites. The project was physically entangled in people's lives. In canton Miandoum there was no way to escape it.

The challenge for the consortium was to keep people who could not be relocated out of the way of its operations while simultaneously showing that its operations had minimal impact on the region, whereas the challenge for residents was how to live alongside the project. The *EMP* was supposed to offset the anticipated effects of the consortium's presence on local communities. In this book, I frame the consortium's adoption of global standards and the risk mitigation policies in the *EMP* not as a defensive response to a World Bank mandate or pressure from activists, or even as a quid pro quo for the World Bank's cover, but as an embrace of a form of global governance that encompasses state and nonstate actors, including corporations and multiple sources of regulatory authority (Shamir 2010). The *EMP* incorporated standards and best practices from a dizzying array of sources, including the World Bank, the Organisation for Economic Co-operation and Development, the International Labor Organization, the U.S. Environmental Protection Agency, the American National Standards Institute, the American Water Works Association, the Mine Safety and Health Administration, the American Conference of Governmental Industrial Hygienists, the International Union for the Conservation of Nature, the World Health Organization, the Basel Convention on the Control of Transboundary Movements of Hazardous Wastes and their Disposal, and the oil and gas industry.

Since the 1980s, global corporations, especially in the extractive sector, have proactively adopted social and environmental standards (Hilson 2012). Along with the World Bank, they have made a "business case" for corporate social responsibility, or CSR (World Bank, n.d.-b; 2013). The CSR movement is fueled by the idea that companies will act in their own "enlightened self-interest" and that their actions will, as Callisto Madavo said at the groundbreaking ceremony, "bring them good returns but also . . . improve African society at large." Transnational policy regimes that include performance standards, environmental assessment, monitoring, and audit are now widespread in extractive industry projects, including projects without World Bank financing (Li 2009).

Standards are guides for ethical conduct but the question of how to demonstrate ethical behavior is complicated in oil projects. As Catherine Dolan and

Dinah Rajak (2011) have argued, companies do not simply extend universal ethics to the different sites where they operate. Instead, ethics take shape in specific localities, within the particularities of a place. In Chad, the EMP was the guidebook for corporate ethics and it brought together the consortium's interests; anthropological knowledge of kinship, local ecologies, and systems of land tenure in the oil field region; Chadian law; and many other threads. One of the threads I emphasize throughout this book is what Jamie Cross (2011) has referred to as a corporate ethic of detachment, which refers to the propensity of companies, and perhaps especially global oil companies, to work to truncate commitments along their global supply chains. In the oil field region this included obligations and responsibilities to the farmers whose land was needed for the project. The EMP and the consortium's claims of ethical conduct were contested and, as in other oil projects, these claims had to be continuously demonstrated (Barry 2013), which the consortium tried to do by regularly reporting on its consultation with local residents, on the critiques of NGOs and project monitors, and on its responses to those critiques.

My analysis of how the risk mitigation policies worked is anchored in what Candace Vogler has called "complex scenes." These are scenes in which people find themselves "often with very little determinate practical orientation and no especially coherent basis for making sense of their situations" (2002, 627). But there they are. A recurring feeling I had while doing fieldwork was that I was witnessing people who were confronted with dilemmas, choices, problems, and opportunities they had never encountered or imagined. They regularly struggled with how to act and what to do. These complex scenes provide entry points to explore the transformational capacities of model policies without taking those capacities as given or determinate. The analysis of complex scenes highlights the creative potential of people and of policy to shape new social imaginaries and self-representations and new ideas about how to live.

There were many actors in the scenes I witnessed. As Cris Shore and Susan Wright (1997) point out, neoliberal reforms do not mean less government, and a broad array of state and nonstate actors were active in facilitating the implementation of the pipeline project. Impact assessments, monitoring, audit, and participatory mechanisms like "community consultation" and public review of project documents are critical technologies of governance, and they are carried out with the help of experts, professional consultants, academics, and local intermediaries (Barry 2013; Li 2009). The profusion of actors in the governance of extractive projects makes it difficult, as it did in Chad, to distinguish the functions and identities of the people and institutions involved in governing or to tell who is doing what (Barry 2004).

The consortium created different classes of intermediaries and charged them with responsibility for a range of state-like functions that smoothed the implementation of extractive activities, such as signing contracts, demarcating boundaries, witnessing payments, managing grievances, and adjudicating disputes. The consortium also performed state-like functions itself: it set and enforced speed limits and traffic rules on public roads, created land registries for the villages of the oil field region, and allocated rights in land in places where the state was unable to document land claims or to make those claims formal or legal. Anthropologists have come to play particularly vital roles in extractive industry projects (Ballard and Banks 2003; Coumans 2011; Guyer 2002, 2011; Welker, Partridge, and Hardin 2011) and they occupied prominent posts in the project in Chad. The World Bank named an academic anthropologist to its principal monitoring body, the IAG (Guyer 2002, 2011), and the consortium hired a consultant who later became a staff anthropologist to interface with local populations and to conduct fieldwork that informed the development of the *Compensation and Resettlement Plan* (Mallaby 2004), the plan governing the expropriation of land.

At the same time, analyzing the implementation of model policies through an analytic of governmentality has severe limitations in an oil extraction project, where force or the threat of force is inescapable. Watts has described oil enclaves as "saturated with all manner of actual and symbolic violence, and the stench of security and surveillance" (2004a, 61). In the oil field region, coercion was always lurking behind what appeared to be participatory or consensual processes. Private security companies were the main employers in the region, and thousands of private security guards, backed up by state security forces, patrolled the roads and guarded the consortium's installations. The dense web of security contained people's movements and pressed in on them literally as well as figuratively, so that opportunities to self-govern were not always experienced as liberating or even as choices (Shore and Wright 1997) but instead as mandates to be enforced if necessary.

The state played a vital role in enforcing the consortium's policies. This book joins a growing body of work on governance in sites of extraction that challenges depictions of the African state as weak, receding, or absent. In fact, global oil companies rely on the state to clear the way for extractive activities, and states are even contractually obligated by global oil companies to do so. Global oil companies hold the state accountable for maintaining order, and they impose penalties for work stoppages or delays due to strikes, boycotts, or protests (Friends of the Earth, n.d.). The terms of Chad's agreements with ExxonMobil included a stability clause preventing the Chadian government from impinging on ExxonMobil's "rights and economic benefits" and stipulating that their convention trumped Chadian law (Coll 2012, 160). Amnesty International (2005) has highlighted the consortium's use of these kinds of technical and legal mechanisms to compel the state to make it illegal for people to "interfere" with the construction, operation, and maintenance of the pipeline, and expressed concerns about the implications of these agreements for freedom of expression and human rights in Chad. One of the obvious effects of the contractual obligations binding the state and the consortium was that the security and administrative functions of the state were highly visible in the oil field region even as the developmental state and state-sponsored social services remained absent.

The policies in the EMP, the representations of local culture and social organization that underpinned them, and the consortium's efforts to distance and detach itself from long-term commitments to the region and the recovery and rehabilitation of local populations were hotly contested, especially by residents. The consortium did not attempt to stifle the critiques of the EMP or reports of its noncompliance with the EMP by project monitors. In fact, as Barry (2013) has suggested, oil companies anticipate these critiques and they work to manage them. In Chad the consortium handled critiques about its conduct by showcasing its formal consultation program and by reproducing NGO's complaints and project monitors' critical observations so as to be able to respond to them. Yet lurking in the backdrop and operating simultaneously to enforce compliance with the EMP were 'harder' governmental mechanisms: contracts, stability clauses, and the threat of (state) force.

At the Heart of the Continent

On April 11, 2001, shortly after I started fieldwork for this project, I was listening to *Morning Edition* on National Public Radio. The host, Bob Edwards, was introducing Paul Raeburn, a senior writer for *Business Week*. Raeburn had just returned from a trip to Chad and had recorded a commentary for NPR on "new trends for business endeavors in developing countries." The commentary was a paean to the oil industry packaged as a set of reflections on the first six months of the pipeline project. What caught my ear, though, was how Raeburn depicted Chad and the oil field region. He described Chad as "a large, wind-scrubbed rectangle of land," and said that the people of southern Chad "live a nineteenth-century, pre-industrial life." According to Raeburn, Chad was disconnected from the world and the global economy, the people who lived there were living in another time, and the project was going to change that (National Public Radio 2001).

Raeburn's commentary was remarkable not for its parochialism or its observations on business trends but for how it aligned with the narrative about Chad that had become standard in the lead-up to the project. The World Bank justified its support for the project by writing, in a text posted to its website, that Chad was among the "poorest of the poor" and "had few options for improving its plight," since "only about 3 percent of the land is fit for growing crops" (World Bank, n.d.-a). As James Ferguson argued in *The Anti-Politics Machine* (1994), development discourse constructs its object in specific ways for specific purposes. In portraying Chad as a lost cause with no resources other than oil, using claims that were empirically inaccurate, the World Bank and the consortium were able to make a case for the pipeline project as the only way forward. The notion that oil was Chad's hope for escaping poverty was widely shared in and outside Chad, but as activists noted in the lead-up to the World Bank's approval of the project, the model or the World Bank's formulation of the project was not inevitable.

The image of the oil field region that emerged from the plans in the *EMP* was of a place where nothing happened before the project arrived. As part of the *Compensation and Resettlement Plan,* which makes up one volume of the *EMP,* the consortium published maps of the oil field region that depict the region as a collection of dispersed villages along with a few rivers and minor roads. But the dominant feature of the maps is empty space.[9] The consortium (as the author of the *EMP*) and journalists like Raeburn suggested that people merely existed there, scratching out a living on land they were unable to put to more productive use and waiting passively for something that would change their lives. At a hearing of the House Subcommittee on Africa that I attended in April 2002, Tom Walters, then ExxonMobil's vice president for oil development in Africa, said, "We have the opportunity of applying this model on a clean slate. . . . There was no prior history of development to deal with" (Coll 2012, 164). In *Private Empire,* a penetrating account of ExxonMobil, Steve Coll writes about the uncharacteristic zeal with which the company approached the project in Chad—a place it thought of as virgin territory. Coll quotes Rex Tillerson, now the company's president, as describing the project as "a clean sheet of paper" and as saying that ExxonMobil had "the opportunity to put things in place perhaps the way you'd like to see them carried out from the very beginning" (2012, 164). This idea of Chad as a void and the oil field region as *terra nullius* and a place where nothing happened before the project arrived was also given clear expression in the speech delivered by Madavo, the World Bank's representative, at the groundbreaking ceremony in Komé:

> As an African, too, I am heartened by the sheer size of this private investment at the heart of our continent—which needs to attract much more international capital if we are to realize our development dreams. And I can almost feel the burden of those thirty years you have been waiting here in Chad—since this oil was first discovered—being lifted from your shoulders now.

These images and references to a region and a people separated and isolated from the world—"at the heart of our continent"—have political effects (Gupta and Ferguson 1992; Massey 2005). For instance, the idea that land in the oil field region "belongs to the state" (Guyer 2002), while technically descriptive of colonial-era land laws, was not a neutral claim. It paved the way for the consortium to take land while limiting compensation to farmers for "improvements" to the land. It also fed the imaginary of farmers in the oil field region as "dwellers in nature"—as people who lived beyond the reach of cadastral services and other modern institutions in a precontact state of isolation (Grovogui and Leonard 2007, 57). These images and references depoliticized and even naturalized expropriation by describing farmers as shifting from plot to plot seasonally, without any particular attachment to the land they worked. In the consortium's plan for expropriation, farmers' plots were described as interchangeable; one plot could be replaced by any other. The only exceptions were settlements and sites identified as "cultural property." By marking off some land as collective and outside the sphere of the market, as an "inalienable possession" (Weiner 1992) to which people had topophilic attachments (Tuan 1990), the rest appears unmarked and unclaimed, and therefore available for the taking.

Other stories—stories that highlight interconnection rather than separation and isolation—could have been told. Land in the oil field region "belongs to the state" because in the early decades of the twentieth century colonial governments in Africa brought as much land as possible under administrative control and not, as the consortium suggested, because of deep and distinctive cultural differences in person-land relations between Africans and Europeans or North Americans.[10] In French Equatorial Africa, the French converted land that the colonial administration defined as "unused and unoccupied" (*terres vacant et sans maître*) into state property (Njoh 2000) and allocated it to concessionary companies to support the colonial administration and supply Europe with raw materials. Concessionary companies found southern Chad unattractive (Thompson and Adloff 1960), leading colonial administrators to adopt a policy of mandatory cotton cultivation to generate revenues for the colonial state. Far from being a clean slate on which there was no prior history of development to deal with, the south of Chad was radically transformed by this intervention (Magnant 1986) in ways that continued to reverberate in the time of oil.

The system of cotton cultivation that the colonial administration put in place altered the geography of the south and of canton Miandoum. Colonial authorities created villages and changed patterns of land use in ways that complicated claims to land and to compensation in the time of the project. The policy of mandatory cotton cultivation led to a dramatic expansion of the cash economy, rapid deforestation, and changes in the local ecology, soil conditions, and conditions of food security (Cabot 1965). In recent years, the drop in world cotton prices, which is directly tied to the payment of subsidies to cotton growers in the United States and the European Union, has led to a sharp decline in cotton production in Chad (CotonTchad 2012). The semiprivatization of the national cotton company, CotonTchad, that was carried out as part of economic reforms imposed by the World Bank, has shifted risks onto individual growers (Magrin 2001). By the time the pipeline project started, most families in the oil field region had abandoned cotton production because it was too risky and unpredictable. They relied instead on staple grains and other food crops to meet their needs for food and cash, and they farmed on depleted soils and dwindling reserves of land.

In fact, Esso's history in Chad and Firmin's family's experience of caring for Conoco's test well were themselves reflections of Chad's implication in the world system before market liberalization and export production became favored development prescriptions. The long wait for oil in canton Miandoum was bound up with the nature and location of Chadian oil, which also had implications for the way the project unfolded. Over the life of the project, the consortium expanded its operations well beyond what it had envisioned in its initial blueprints. Between 2005 and 2009 it developed four additional oil fields, including three oil fields in the OFDA—the Nya, Maikeri, and Timbré oil fields—and the Moundouli oil field outside the boundaries of the original oil field region. In response to lower-than-expected production figures, the consortium also initiated an infill drilling program and added hundreds of additional wells in the oil field region, so that by the end of 2012 a total of 895 wells, instead of 287, were expected to be in operation (ECMG 2012, 62). The expansion of the project and the addition of project infrastructure swelled the consortium's land requirements. The consortium expropriated more than double the 2,124 hectares it originally estimated would be needed for the project (EEPCI 1999b, vol. 3, sec. 3.2).

In explaining the need to expand the project, the consortium pointed to lagging production figures. Production was lower than expected due to "a challenging and unusual combination of geologic issues" that required a series of costly "enhancement procedures" (EEPCI 2008a, 7). The addition of more wells was one of those enhancements and was supposed to allow the consortium to tap into the "meandering" and discontinuous layers of oil-bearing sands in the extinct river channels of the Doba basin. A program of "frequent well stimulations" that involved "back washing" the wells was implemented to unclog the pores in the sands and increase the flow of oil. The consortium also built a high-pressure water injection system to increase reservoir pressure, which declines with production in most oil fields but declined more rapidly than the consortium expected in the Doba basin fields (EEPCI 2008a, 8). Yet, even with these production enhancements, the project produced roughly 100,000 to 130,000 barrels of oil per day—far short of preproject projections of 225,000 barrels per day.

The consortium also explained the project's expansion in terms of the properties of the crude oil in the Doba basin. "Doba blend" is the name for the mixture of crude collected from the different Doba basin fields. It is a heavy, viscous crude that has low mobility and high levels of calcium and acids. The market for high acid crudes, which are known in the industry as high total acid number (high TAN) crudes, is limited because they are expensive to process. High TAN crudes are corrosive and require specialized refining equipment or have to be blended with other crudes that have fewer impurities before they can be processed. An industry publication underscored this point in a piece titled "Doba Finds a Home" about the opening of a refinery in Wales that had to be retrofitted to receive Chadian oil at a cost of $12 million (Kelly 2004). Doba blend is said to have "an unusually high TAN" (Energy Sector Management Assistance Programme 2005) and is what industry experts call a "challenged crude," because under normal refining operations only one-fifth of a barrel can be transformed into high-value products such as gasoline, diesel, or jet fuel, compared to two-thirds of a barrel for the benchmark Brent crude (EEPCI 2005b; Inkpen and Moffett 2011). Over the life of the project, the discount for Doba blend relative to the standard Brent crude ranged from two dollars per barrel, when only oil from the Miandoum field was flowing through the pipeline, to nearly twenty dollars per barrel once the other oil fields with lower quality crudes were also brought online (Energy Sector Management Assistance Programme 2005; Inkpen and Moffett 2011).

The development of new technologies for exploration and extraction has made the recovery of oil feasible under an increasingly wide range of conditions (Barry 2013; Watts 2005). As the market for oil expands, small deposits, low-quality crude, and isolated or challenging field sites like Chad's Doba basin have become more attractive to global oil companies. ExxonMobil was well aware that it needed to expand its operations in so-called weak states if it wanted to maintain its level of reserves (Coll 2012). But the complications and high costs of producing "challenged crude" in unstable places are also reflected in the benefits of oil to producing countries. The royalty rate Chad receives for its oil has ranged from 12.5 to 14.25 percent of the sale value of a barrel of oil. This is lower than the royalty rates negotiated by almost all other African oil producers, and Chad's actual rate of return is even lower, since the rate is applied only after the consortium has deducted a transportation surcharge of roughly ten dollars per barrel for transporting the oil to market through the pipeline (EEPCI 2008a; Gary and Reisch 2005). The high costs of recovering low-quality crude in a poor country with "a challenging and unusual combination of geologic issues" are only some of the reasons Chad and other African oil producers are unable to negotiate favorable terms with global oil companies (Appel 2012; Gary and Karl 2003; Hilson 2012). The World Bank's proposal to provide negotiating training to Chadian officials as part of the *Petroleum Sector Management Capacity Building Project* fails to take these reasons for poor oil deals into account and treats the matter as a managerial one to be addressed through the development of soft skills.

The pipeline project entered a region that was already thoroughly entangled in the world system and in hierarchical relations of power, and not a place "where there was no prior history of development to deal with." What Raeburn encountered on his trip to the oil field region were the effects of the twentieth century, and not the failure of time to touch that part of the world. Akhil Gupta and James Ferguson have noted that "if one begins with the premise that spaces have *always* been hierarchically interconnected, instead of naturally disconnected, then cultural and social change becomes not a matter of cultural contact and articulation but one of rethinking difference *through* connection" (1992, 8, emphasis in the original). The pipeline project was just one in a long series of efforts to extract profit from the south of Chad, the region colonial officials referred to as *le Tchad utile*, "useful Chad."

The story of the long wait for oil in canton Miandoum is not usually told as a story about global oil markets or how Chad's "challenged crude" and its complex geography and geology and landlocked position on the continent have become more attractive to multinational oil companies as they struggle to find replacement oil in the midst of dwindling reserves and a worldwide oil rush (Gold and Gonzalez 2011). It is told instead as a story about Chad as a place that was dangerous and unpredictable, and too risky for investors before the World Bank came on the scene. "With Chad's history of civil war, ethnic strife and corruption, its oil lay untapped for decades because no one was willing to put capital at risk here," declared a pair of journalists writing for the *New York Times* (Polgreen and Dugger 2006). A World Bank official said the bank invested in the project because "it represented an exceptional opportunity for Chad to use the oil revenues to make up for the developmental delays accumulated during the periods of internal conflicts" (Tcheyan 2003). By these accounts, the story of the long wait for oil in canton Miandoum was not about global oil companies needing Chad but about Chad needing global oil companies.

Life in the Time of Oil

From the time the pipeline project started through the end of 2012, I spent at least three months in the oil field region each year. I spent most of that time in four of the now forty-eight villages in canton Miandoum, one of three cantons that were ground zero for the pipeline project. Although I did not know it when I started the project, the consortium would come to array these villages at different points along a continuum that was supposed to capture the project's impact in different parts of the oil field region. The consortium classified the village of Ngalaba, which later split to form two villages, called Ngalaba 1 and Ngalaba 2, as a high-impact village, while the villages of Maikeri and Bendoh, the other villages where I focused my fieldwork, were classified as moderate- and low-impact villages. These classifications were based on the proportion of the village land base the consortium took for the project and villages shifted status over time as the consortium's land needs expanded and contracted.

In each village I followed a subset of families, eighty families in total. There were no particular criteria used to select the families other than their willingness to be visited regularly for an indefinite period of time, although they were selected to avoid enlisting only a few extended family clusters. I had year-round assistance from fieldworkers who lived in canton Miandoum and who helped me keep up on events in the oil field region when I was away. We collected a wide assortment of information about the families through interviews, observations, measurements, and surveys. We maintained a household census and kept track of people's movements, and we collected information on land use practices, sources of income, expenses, household assets, agricultural production practices, the uses of compensation payments, conflicts over land, illnesses, causes of death, diets, and food security. We collected stories about the founding of the villages and wrote village histories, inventoried farm equipment and animals, and measured the fertility of the soils in family fields. The eclecticism of the information resembles what Clifford Geertz has called "convergent data":

> By convergent data I mean descriptions, measures, observations, what you will, which are at once diverse, even rather miscellaneous, both as to type and degree of precision and generality, unstandardized facts, opportunistically collected and variously portrayed, which yet turn out to shed light on one another for the simple reason that the individuals they are descriptions, measures, or observations of are directly involved in one another's lives. (Geertz 1983, 156)

Geertz's concept of convergent data might seem anachronistic in a time when it is understood that communities are not the bounded, close-knit, and insular localities that were the mainstay of earlier anthropological fieldwork. But I used the material to locate and track the movement of the standards regime in the routines of daily life and not to build a description of some coherent, cultural whole. I looked for "complex scenes"—for contests over how to live or moments when the model disrupted people's daily routines and turned them into subjects of discussion, debate, and negotiation. The formal data collection exercises register only faintly in this book because they were accompanied and superseded by attempts to follow complex scenes as they unfolded over time. I spent most of my time following domestic disputes, feuds between families, and the latest controversies in the villages. People asked for help in communicating with the consortium, nongovernmental organizations (NGOs), and human rights organizations. They sought advice about what to say in response to the consortium's queries or they wanted to share their worries and preoccupations or their side of a story. Documents were the focus of many of our exchanges. The project generated copious amounts of paper: letters, contracts, certificates, convocations, and announcements were shared, copied, debated, and discussed. The stories that emerged from these encounters opened out onto other scenes and put me in contact with other families, local authorities, consortium staff, activists who worked with NGOs in regional capitals, N'Djamena and beyond, project monitors, and World Bank employees in N'Djamena and Washington, DC.

The chapters in this book focus on specific aspects of the standards regime and show how some of the "bits and pieces" of the model were described and enacted (Peck and Theodore 2010, 170), what kinds of people and practices made them operational, and what they produced in the oil field region and, ultimately, beyond it. In chapter 2, "Dead Letters," I offer an account of the workings of the grievance mechanism that was established to address residents' complaints. Residents thought of the letters they wrote to the consortium as "dead" because they went unanswered, but I show how letter writing and the intermediaries who helped residents produce letters taught them what claims the consortium could recognize and recorded those claims in durable form, which had the effect of literally writing the project into their lives.

In chapter 3, "Becoming Eligible," I show how the consortium's efforts to terminate ongoing obligations to residents of the oil field region shaped involuntary resettlement. The consortium devolved responsibility for resettlement and the rehabilitation of farmers to others, and especially to farmers themselves. Resettlement policies created new categories of farmers. Those who became eligible for resettlement (*les éligibles*) were not necessarily the most land poor but those who could demonstrate entrepreneurialism and resourcefulness—the same capacities that retraining programs were supposed to help them acquire. Farmers eventually became so successful at becoming eligible for resettlement that they provoked a public relations crisis and forced the consortium to reengage, though in ways that further complicated farmers' efforts to recover and restore their livelihoods.

The consortium implemented the *Land Use Mitigation Action Plan,* or LUMAP, in 2007 in response to the public relations crisis spurred by the expansion of the project and the expropriation of additional land. In chapter 4, "Ties That Bind," I examine how the creation of comprehensive village land registries and land-mapping exercises that required farmers to stake exclusive claims to plots of land transformed kinship, familial relations and social networks in ways that were deeply gendered while expediting land transfer operations and producing data the consortium could use to shape media coverage of the project.

The consortium distributed nonhazardous waste in local communities as part of a community recycling program, but the status of the objects in circulation was always ambiguous ("property" or "waste"?) and therefore so was the status of the people who possessed those objects ("thieves" or "beneficiaries"?). In chapter 5, "In the Midst of Things," I show how the consortium's protocols for managing material and equipment as property and as waste transformed the entire oil field region, including nonproject sites, into a space of surveillance. The anticipation of raids, road blocks, check points, and house-to-house searches reconfigured the geography of people's movements and their relationships with project-related things and kept them off the roads and away from work sites.

As an experiment in development, the pipeline project ended in 2008 with the World Bank's announcement of its withdrawal from the project. But the model lives on. Chapter 6, "Footprints," takes the form of an epilogue. I look at the ways the World Bank and the consortium narrated the experiment and its effects and I propose, in contrast, that standards and risk mitigation policies contained disputes, kept residents out of the way, ordered the circulation of people and things in the oil field region, and shifted responsibilities for rehabilitation onto those who were displaced so the project could move forward at breakneck speed while appearing to have no impact on local populations. I suggest that the model was not an antidote to the resource curse but that it instead helped to produce it.

TWO

Dead Letters

Mbairo Justin emerged from his house with a worn copy of a letter, which he handed to me. It was dated July 3, 2001 and was written by hand in tight, careful lines on a single piece of paper. The letter was addressed to "those in charge of the office of compensation at Esso,"[1] and the purpose of the letter was declared at the top of the page. "*Objet:* Clarification of the role of the chief of the canton in the amount of compensation paid for fruit trees." This was followed by one long paragraph in which Mbairo explained that on the same day the consortium paid him 550,000 francs for a mango tree it had inadvertently destroyed with a backhoe, the chief of the canton "grabbed" the money and told him he would have to wait six months to receive it. Five months later, the chief called Mbairo to his house, where—over Mbairo's objections—he divided the money among five people. The names of the recipients were listed in the letter, along with the amounts each person received. The chief gave Mbairo 100,000 francs. He took 50,000 francs for himself, and put another 30,000 francs into a fund for the village. Three other men split the balance of the payment. Mbairo closed the letter by pleading with the consortium. "Find me a solution," he wrote, "because the chief of the canton is ready to send me to jail."

For most of the duration of the pipeline project, the oil field region was awash in letters. People who could write were besieged with requests to compose or to copy letters. Human rights organizations were inundated with duplicates of letters people had sent to the consortium or, less frequently, to the World Bank. Mbairo's letter was copied to six recipients. People kept copies of their letters and showed them to anyone they thought might be able to intervene on their behalf or push their case forward. People wrote to complain that the consortium destroyed their crops and trees without paying compensation, that jobs had been unfairly distributed, that there were no business opportunities, that compensation was paid to the wrong person, that the rates were insufficient or were calculated incorrectly, or that local authorities took their payments. "Information" was the *objet* of many letters. The purpose of writing was to pass along a piece of important or disturbing news. "I am informing you that David Terrassement [a subcontractor] is uprooting trees and the owners have filed claims but they have not had any response." The consortium's failure to respond to a previous letter became, in itself, something to write about. Letters begot more letters.

What was striking about the letters, apart from the fact that many of the people who sent letters could not read or write them, was that most of them went unanswered. No one I knew who wrote a letter ever received one in return, and by 2004 or 2005 few letters generated a response of any kind. This massive outpouring of words was met by almost complete silence. If people initially anticipated that their letters would prompt the consortium to take action or lead to some form of redress, they quickly learned not to expect anything at all. They wondered aloud what the consortium did with their letters, and derisively suggested that they used them for toilet paper or just threw them in the trash. People described their letters as *lettres morts*—dead letters. But they kept writing. I remember asking a group of men who were talking about a recent letter why they kept writing when no one replied and no one expected a reply. They stared at me blankly. After a long pause, one of them said, matter-of-factly, "We have to write." His friends nodded in agreement.

People produced the letters in response to the consortium's grievance mechanism. The grievance mechanism was not a mandatory feature of the project, but the consortium followed the World Bank's advice in setting one up.[2] The World Bank recommends that borrowers establish grievance mechanisms to manage what it refers to as "operational risks" (World Bank, n.d.-b, 2; World Bank 2013). Grievance mechanisms are supposed to allow operators to identify and address grievances early, before communities coalesce around project-related complaints or protests erupt, resulting in costly delays and disruptions. The World Bank makes a "business case" for grievance mechanisms, but it also describes grievance mechanisms as mechanisms for extending due process to people in places where the state is thought of as absent or its authority as so attenuated that it is not possible for people to obtain justice through the legal system (Compliance Advisor/Ombudsman 2008). Extractive enclaves are often depicted in just this way—as spaces vacated by the state, or as isolated hot spots disconnected and administered separately from the territorial nation-states in which they are located (Ferguson 2005, 2006).

These descriptions often gloss or ignore the ways the state is implicated in the functioning of extractive enclaves. By foregrounding the absence of the formal machinery of the state, these descriptions also ignore other forms of regulation that structure life in these spaces (Adunbi 2011; Sawyer 2004; Watts 2004a; Zalik 2004). Rolph Trouillot (2001, 2003) has argued that the practices of nongovernmental organizations (NGOs), multinational companies, and transnational organizations like the International Monetary Fund and the World Bank can produce effects as powerful as those produced by nation-states. He describes a number of these "state effects," including isolation, identification, legibility, and spatialization effects, whose emergence in the oil field region I trace through an ethnographic look at the functioning of the grievance mechanism the consortium put in place. In this chapter, I am interested in the grievance mechanism as a mode of administration in the oil field region—in how it worked, the effects it had, the interactions people had with it, and what people made of it and of the technologies it introduced.

I suggest that the grievance mechanism *domesticated disputes* while at the same time transforming residents of the oil field region into individual claimants, landowners, middle figures, and bureaucrats and providing them with technologies—notably letters—to record their claims and to project them into the future. These were interrelated facets of the grievance mechanism as a mode of administration. Disputes were domesticated in two senses: they were tamed, and they were sequestered in villages and domestic spaces where they had to be managed. Intermediaries were critical to these processes. Disputes were tamed because the grievance mechanism required people to frame their complaints narrowly. I show how consortium employees known as local community contacts (LCCs), NGO activists, and local authorities vetted their letters and mediated their communications with the consortium. In coaching people to write letters that would be legible to the consortium, in triaging their claims, and in receiving and selectively processing their letters on behalf of the consortium, these intermediaries became comanagers of the project. In this way, the grievance mechanism contained disputes in villages and domestic spaces, far from the extractive activities of the consortium.

People wrote to mobilize the consortium to take action on their behalf, but they continued writing, and even picked up the pace of writing, as the probability of receiving a response receded. The persistent fervor to write suggests that the consortium's response to claims was not the only thing at stake for letter writers. When I probed people about their motives for writing, I got responses, like the one above, that were opaque and impossible to decipher. But when I paid attention to the letters themselves, it became apparent that they were not "dead" even if the consortium never responded to them. In fact, they were quite productive. The letters did not turn out concrete solutions to the problems people wrote about, but they inscribed the project throughout the oil field region. *They wrote the project into life.* This happened in two ways. People wrote, reproduced, and disseminated the consortium's policies through the medium of letters, and letters were documents that wrote the project into life by their material presence. The letters naturalized the language and logics the consortium introduced and made them a part of everyday life. They also functioned as handwritten certificates of title that transformed farmers into private landowners even in the absence of courts of law or cadastral offices. They served as "official" records of land claims and established individual farmers as having exclusive rights to property in an environment of growing land scarcity and competition for dwindling resources.

The Rules of Letter Writing

The first person to receive a copy of Mbairo's letter was the consortium's local community contact, or LCC. According to the World Bank, grievance mechanisms should include an accessible "focal point" where people can register their complaints (World Bank, n.d.-b), and the LCCs—who were hired by the consortium to act as liaisons between the oil companies and residents of the oil field region— served this function. One LCC was posted to each canton in which the consortium was active, and this person was the first, and sometimes the only, point of contact residents had with the consortium (Barclay and Koppert 2007). LCCs had to be from the oil field region, and they had to speak French, have a high school diploma, and pass a competitive exam. Because of these requirements, the people selected to fill the posts were typically young men in their twenties and thirties who had spent several years attending school in regional towns and cities before returning to their villages to take up farming.

The LCCs worked out of satellite offices in the *chef-lieu*—the village that was the commercial and administrative hub for the canton. The satellite offices were repurposed grain storage sheds or small, one-room buildings. Most were located along the main road or were easily identified by a large Esso sign that was attached to the side of the building or to a stick planted in the dirt at the building's entrance. The creation of satellite offices was supposed to facilitate regular communication with residents, but it also kept residents away from the consortium's main base camp, which was the operational nerve center for the project and was where expatriate employees and a few Chadians worked and lived in trailers. The camp was built in an isolated spot in the middle of agricultural land, but as soon as it opened, people waiting for jobs formed a settlement just across the road that soon morphed into a sprawling village.[3] The consortium's camp, which was referred to as Komé Base or just "the base," was fenced off and heavily secured and was off-limits to everyone except consortium employees and visitors on official business.

People from the canton stopped by the LCCs' satellite offices to ask questions about the project and to file grievances. In fact, one of the main responsibilities of the LCCs was to receive people's grievances and to work with consortium staff and local authorities to evaluate and manage them.[4] The consortium provided an account of how this was supposed to work in its *Compensation and Resettlement Plan* (EEPCI 1999b), which said that farmers were to be informed of their right to grieve when they signed land transfer contracts ceding their land to the consortium. People could file written claims with the consortium or they could make oral statements to consortium staff if they were accompanied by the chief of their village. Claims related to the payment of compensation were to be resolved within the same agricultural cycle, while those for damages, such as to crops and trees, had to be signaled while the damage was still visible, and therefore followed a tighter timeline. The consortium pledged to track the complaints people registered and to make changes to their operations based on the patterns that emerged.

At the beginning of the pipeline project, the LCCs found the consortium's policies confusing and this part of their job tricky and time-consuming. I spent a lot of time talking to the LCCs in their satellite offices and listening to them describe the difficulties they had managing both the complaints and their relationships with friends, neighbors, and family members, who had as much trouble as they did making sense of the policies and were angry and frustrated by the loss of land, the lack of jobs, and the one-time payments. The LCCs told me they had studied the *Compensation and Resettlement Plan,* but that even after reading and rereading the relevant passages they still had difficulty understanding the consortium's definitions or following their logic and they had to ask their supervisors to parse the text. The consortium established reading rooms (*salles de lecture*) in towns around the oil field region where people could consult the plan and other policy documents. But the documents were dense and technical, and the reading rooms were almost always empty. The consortium also held community consultation sessions during which consortium staff, accompanied by the LCCs, described the compensation and resettlement process, the lottery system used to distribute jobs, and the grievance mechanism people could use to file complaints if they felt they had been treated unfairly. People attended these sessions and listened to the presentations. They found some of the proposals strange and confusing and others made them angry. They went to the satellite offices to ask the LCCs for clarification, to watch demonstrations of how the lottery system worked, and to complain.

When the LCCs received grievance letters they were supposed to evaluate farmers' claims and classify them as *fondée* or *non-fondée*—founded or unfounded. If a farmer alleged that the consortium had damaged his fields or trees without paying compensation, the LCCs were supposed to accompany him to the scene and investigate. In other cases, the LCCs assessed farmers' claims by calling in witnesses, receiving testimony, or gathering other kinds of evidence. Both the LCCs and farmers learned about the consortium's policies through these encounters. They learned what forms claims could take, what types of grievances the consortium would recognize, when grievances had to be filed, and who could file them. Initially, the LCCs undertook the task of investigating farmers' claims with enthusiasm, but their interest in these discovery operations waned as they came to know the consortium's policies and to refer to them as *nos principes*—or our principles. It is difficult to pinpoint exactly when this transformation began or ended, but by late 2004 or early 2005 it was virtually complete. The LCCs' adoption of the plural possessive pronoun marked a turning point. It signaled the LCCs' newfound facility with the consortium's ideas and their developing understanding of themselves as different from other residents of the oil field region. It marked the moment when the LCCs became middle figures.

Nancy Hunt (1999) describes middle figures as people who internalize and project the civilizing hierarchies embedded in modernizing projects. Middle figures make active claims to an identity as a "middle," and they do this, in part, by differentiating themselves from their "lows" (Hunt 1999, 8). In the discussions I had with LCCs, they readily took up neoliberal critiques of the welfare state when talking about the friends, neighbors, and family members they were supposed to represent. They complained that when people received payments they squandered the money on alcohol and women and continued "to count on assistance" from the project. They claimed that "a virus of laziness" was spreading through the oil field region and that crop yields were declining because the possibility of capturing a windfall payment made farmers too lazy to weed or properly tend to their fields. The LCCs accused people of using tricks instead of industry to win compensation, and told stories about farmers who planted crops on land that had already been marked off for expropriation, who fabricated damage to crops and trees, and who tried to convince the consortium that fallowed land was a "field" in order to capture compensation. The LCCs described these contested plots as *champs piégées,* or fields on which farmers had set traps (*les pièges*) for the consortium. The LCCs' supervisors talked about farmers in the same way. When I met the consortium's *Environmental Management Plan* (*EMP*) manager at Esso's headquarters in N'Djamena, he told me that 90 percent of the grievances farmers filed were *non-fondée* and that most claims were for *champs piégées.*

The transformation of the LCCs into middle figures coincided with a surge in letter writing. Residents of the oil field region also learned how the consortium's policies worked, and they scrambled to capture compensation payments and project benefits. People cleared as much land as they could—often more land than they could cultivate—because only land that was cleared was considered a field and entitled the person who cleared it to a compensation payment. People were especially eager to lay claim to trees and to wooded plots because, according to the consortium's formulas, these brought the largest windfall payments. People studied the movements of project vehicles and tried to anticipate where the consortium would take land next, but they often miscalculated and worked land where the consortium had planted surveyors' stakes with the hope that the consortium would still pay.[5] Filing grievances became one of many ways people tried to win compensation for the loss of land, and by 2003 the volume of complaints had swelled from a trickle to a flood.

If the LCCs initially viewed people's letters as neutral presentations of the facts in a case, they quickly came to see them in a different light. The letters confirmed for them their assessments of farmers as stupid or shifty, and the LCCs treated the letters with scorn and derision. They mocked people's claims and made fun of their handwriting, gaps in comprehension, and spelling errors, such as the widespread use of the phonetically derived *walfatte* for the English term *well pad*. In my conversations with them, the LCCs and their supervisors on the EMP team were quick to tell me that in their efforts to settle disputes they had to "leave the book"— by which they meant the *Compensation and Resettlement Plan*—and "go back to African traditions." For instance, in a dispute between a father and his son over compensation for a tree that straddled their fields, the LCC was unable to broker a settlement, but the EMP manager—the same one who told me that 90 percent of farmers' claims were *non-fondée*—described how both parties ceded when he reminded the father that "a father works for his son" and the son that "a son works for his father." Farmers had to be engaged through tradition, parable, and proverb because, as their letters showed, they were immune to book learning or policy logic.

This orientation to farmers and their letters fueled growing tensions between LCCs and the residents they represented. The LCCs' mandate to diffuse *nos principes* combined with their physical proximity to residents made them easy targets for people's anger, frustration, and disappointment with the project. Residents threatened the LCCs for implementing controversial policies, and at least one LCC was physically assaulted by people angered over the lack of jobs and the methods used to fill the few positions available. People were also angry and jealous about the LCCs' rapid rise in wealth and status in their communities and at how they enriched themselves—often at others' expense—by taking bribes and engaging in various forms of graft.[6] My field notes were filled with people's accounts of the ways the LCCs and other members of the EMP's socioeconomic team made money from them by falsifying land transfer contracts and taking money in exchange for jobs. At times, community consultation sessions and public information meetings devolved into shouting matches. One of the meetings I attended broke up prematurely, with insults being hurled in all directions. As the LCCs hurried to their vehicle, an elderly woman shouted after them, "God will judge you for what you are doing!" Even though I attended the meeting as an observer and sat in the back row, the next day I received a garbled but menacing text message from an angry LCC that ended with "Tu auras" (You will get it).

As that text message suggests, my relationship with the LCCs was awkward. Our interactions were fraught, and reflected the difficulties the LCCs experienced trying to navigate their middle positions. On the one hand, I visited the LCCs not only in their offices but also in their homes. I attended a funeral for a family member of one of the LCCS, and I had lunch or drinks with several of the men who occupied these positions. On the other hand, my ambiguous role in the villages was unsettling to them. Ellen Patterson Brown, the consortium's staff anthropologist and the LCCS' supervisor for much of the project period, probed them about my research and what I was doing in the villages. An LCC once approached me at a ceremony to ask why I had come to his house the day before and why I had not announced the purpose of my visit. Had it been a family visit or a professional visit?

The LCCS were supposed to keep a log of visitors and write monthly reports about their activities and the issues and problems they encountered or heard about, and they struggled with how to incorporate our interactions into these formats. My requests for interviews were often preceded by advance work and the assurances of Ngondoloum, a colleague who happened to be related to one of the LCCS. But I was still stood up more than once.

In the early years of the project, the LCCS were visible and accessible to me and to residents, but as the project wore on they became increasingly aloof, distant, and difficult to find. They rarely opened their satellite offices. Their relationships with friends and family became strained, and some of them moved to nearby towns or outside the *chef-lieu* where they worked. They dropped out of social groups or were barred from participating in them because of complaints that they relayed what they saw and heard to their supervisors or the chiefs of the cantons. As the relationship between LCCS and other residents of the oil field region soured, the LCCS became dependent on the consortium and local authorities for their physical protection. The consortium arranged for the LCCS to travel around the canton in Land Cruisers instead of on motorcycles and equipped the LCCS' satellite offices with two-way radios so they could signal the base camp if they needed help or were in danger. In responding to my complaint about the menacing text message, the EMP manager told me that he gave the LCCS instructions to leave meetings at the first sign that villagers were becoming upset or angry. He also arranged for the LCCS to visit villages in groups or to be accompanied by the chief of the canton.

People began to refer to the LCCS as "deputies" of the chiefs of the cantons because they were often seen together and because the LCCS depended heavily on the chiefs for their personal security. Residents complained that the LCCS did not want to hear their complaints, and that they were not independent and had to align themselves with the consortium and local authorities. In meetings with World Bank monitors, the LCCS routinely sided with the consortium and denied or contradicted the claims of their friends, neighbors, and family members. The LCCS felt pressured to take up the side of the consortium and talked openly about this in the early years of the project.

The LCCS' alignment with the consortium in implementing the project was remarkable, but it was never complete. Richard Robinson (1972) wrote that the "bargain of collaboration" between colonial authorities and their indigenous intermediaries could never be too one-sided if intermediaries were to retain their authority. The LCCS had to intervene on behalf of the consortium to keep their jobs, but they also had to strategically bend the rules in order to diffuse residents' anger. I once asked an LCC about rumors that people got jobs only if they paid for them. He first responded with a standard demonstration of how the consortium's lottery system worked. I must have looked skeptical, because immediately after the demonstration he lowered his voice and said that people were not happy with the lottery system and that the consortium's methods for allocating jobs had given him problems. One of the chiefs had seen the lottery demonstration multiple times and had even come to the LCC's office to read his operations manual. Leaning back in his chair, the LCC said, "In the end, I understood what the chief was saying to me and he understood my position. So I gave him five positions that he could fill with his family members." He continued, "I have three cousins working for PRIDE [a subcontractor]. Given our society it's not possible that I have the job I have and don't give some of the jobs to my family members." But he insisted that he filled his jobs with people from the canton: "Every Monday is market day in Bébédjia, and the *commerçants* are walking around out there with money, but none of them have jobs."

The LCCS reserved plum jobs for members of their extended families or people willing to pay for them, and they allotted a certain number of positions to local authorities to distribute or to sell as they pleased. They told key associates how to respond to the consortium's questions so they could be classified as land poor and gain access to resettlement benefits and they helped some farmers win larger compensation payments than they otherwise would have by working with members of the EMP team to falsify the boundaries of the farmers' fields, to exaggerate the number of compensation-generating trees on their plots, or to misclassify trees in favor of more valuable species. The LCCS also diffused farmers' anger by blaming others—especially their anonymous colleagues at the base camp. The LCCS claimed that their supervisors sat on farmers' grievances and that other, more powerful, members of the EMP team were involved in schemes to process the farmers' complaints and pocket their money. In some cases, the LCCS even produced documents from these employees showing that farmers had already been paid for the trees or the crops that were the subjects of their complaints. I watched farmers study with wonderment the computer-generated printouts with their photographs and signatures allegedly attesting to the receipt of large sums of money. The documents left them speechless and confused. Were the LCCS in on the schemes to defraud them, or were they simply reporting on the actions of others over whom they had no control? Were the LCCs passing on their letters and advocating for them, or were they disposing of them in order to shield the consortium from their pesky demands? People were divided over where they should direct their anger and unsure about whom to blame for the fact that their letters remained *sans suite.*

Stamps and Signatures

Before Mbairo's letter could be accepted by the LCC for the canton it had to be countersigned by the chief of his village, who was charged with authenticating Mbairo's claims and endorsing his demand. These countersigned letters had an ambiguous legal status, since village chiefs derive their authority from customary law and local support but do not represent the state or act on behalf of it. In many descriptions of extractive enclaves, the African state is depicted as failed, weak, inconsequential, or simply absent. William Reno has noted that extractive industries need to rely on states for legal contractual authority for their operations, but nothing more, and that political instability can even be beneficial to investors because companies can "gain access to resources" and "improve their market position" if they can manage the risks that come with "weak state capacity" (2001, 205). James Ferguson's (2005, 2006) descriptions of extractive enclaves as cut off or disconnected from their national societies are also premised on the notion of a void filled "inside the fence" by global oil companies that hire mercenaries and private security forces to maintain order and "outside the fence" by "a kind of government by NGO" (2005, 380). But what was striking in the oil field region was the ubiquitous presence of military police, soldiers, chiefs, bureaucrats, and other authority figures and the simultaneous efforts of the consortium to *conjure* the state in its Weberian rational-legal form.

In requiring village chiefs to stamp and sign farmers' letters, and in many other ways, the consortium engaged in a mimicry of the state (Das and Poole 2004). The consortium drew village chiefs into performing an array of state-like functions. It was not uncommon to arrive at a chief's house and have family members tell me he was attending a meeting with consortium officials, or to find the chief waiting for the consortium's vehicle to arrive. The consortium assembled village chiefs to solicit their support for new policies and relied on village chiefs to show them sacred sites, certify land claims, and cosign land transfer contracts. Chiefs were asked to verify the boundaries of villages, cantons, and family fields, and in some cases they were charged with establishing these boundaries and drawing them for the first time. Village chiefs or chiefs of the cantons had to be present when compensation payments were made, and they were tasked with identifying the recipients of compensation payments when there were multiple claims to a plot of land.

While the consortium treated local chiefs as key intermediaries, their relationships with them were complicated. Because local authorities were not directly accountable to the consortium, they were assumed to be susceptible to bribery and other forms of corruption, such as the kind Mbairo alleged in his letter. In fact, the project opened up multiple opportunities for local authorities to earn a living—through official as well as unofficial means. Chiefs were paid by the consortium for their time, but they also sold jobs, imposed a 10 percent "tax" on residents' compensation payments, hoarded high-value project waste, charged families for assistance with dispute resolution, and conspired with consortium employees to defraud the consortium (Cogels and Koppert 2004; IAG 2009). Military police, soldiers, and others who were supposed to secure the region fined people for curfew violations—real and invented. They confiscated motorcycles, extorted money from people for possessing project waste, sold public land, and imposed tolls for the use of roads. In these and other ways, local authorities—some with formal links to the state and some without them—made claims on the wealth created by the project. Rather than seeing these kinds of unregulated activities as evidence of a weak state unable to control events at its territorial margins, they might be read along the lines of Janet Roitman's observations in a different Chadian context as reconstituting state power in ways that make it possible to govern "the literal frontiers of the country, as well as the conceptual frontiers of the economy" (2005, 13; see also Roitman 2004).

During the period of the pipeline project there was a remarkable proliferation of authority figures in the oil field region, even though the state remained withdrawn from the provision of health care, education, sanitation, agricultural extension, and other basic social services. The government, as part of its contract with the consortium, was mandated to prevent people from interfering with the consortium's operations, and dispatched members of the military to the region to support the consortium's private security guards. Administrative posts, security personnel, bureaucrats, and chiefs multiplied. Under the World Bank's tutelage, the Chadian government continued its efforts to decentralize, and repeated rounds of administrative restructuring sent scores of administrators into the oil field region. Bringing government closer to the people was supposed to give local government greater autonomy, and in the time of oil it was also supposed to give residents a voice in decisions about how oil revenues earmarked for the region would be spent. The restructuring became so fine-grained that in some instances there was complete overlap in successive territorial and administrative units. Miandoum, for example, is a canton of forty-eight villages that also became a *sous-préfecture* in 2008. This meant that the *sous-préfet* and his subordinate, the chief of the canton, were charged with governing exactly the same population and the same territory.

The saturation of authority in the oil field region had the effect of extending and consolidating central authority rather than devolving it to the local level (Fessha and Kirkby 2008). Government restructuring expanded the reach and influence of the government in N'Djamena and its emphasis on clearing the way for oil production. The consortium hired the LCCs to act as counterweights to local authorities and to be the main interlocutors with residents and with consortium staff about the project and its effects on the ground. Local authorities, who had been responsible for adjudicating land disputes and other conflicts before the project got underway, were relegated to endorsing their accounts and enforcing the consortium's policies. The letters village chiefs could endorse and the roles they could play in the grievance process were also circumscribed by the proliferation of bureaucratic administration. Local authorities had to move carefully in such densely administered terrain. When a farmer brought a grievance letter to the village chief, the chief had to respond with an eye to how his decision would be received by higher-level authorities to whom the farmer or the consortium might appeal. If village chiefs countersigned letters that misrepresented farmers' losses, took a side in a contested claim, or made demands that went beyond the agreements the consortium signed on to uphold they could be overruled by other authorities who were, literally, just around the corner.

They could also run afoul of these authorities. While village chiefs could not be removed by fiat, since they were not appointed or employed by the state, higher-level authorities could wrest power from them by supporting challenges to their authority from below. The project touched off lively debates in the villages of the oil field region over who was best suited to govern in the time of oil. Many incumbent chiefs were perceived as weak or ineffective and were challenged or overthrown. Alternatively, their rivals established splinter villages, which did not involve moving or physical displacement, since this was impossible in a canton with no unclaimed land. The creation of new villages replicated the logic of decentralization, and involved partitioning existing villages into smaller and smaller governing units. Half of the 48 villages in canton Miandoum are actually villages within villages. Their names—Karwa 1 and 2; Bekia 1, 2, 3, and 4; and Kairaty (1)1, (1)2, (1)3, and 2—reflect ongoing struggles for power and authority as well as the scramble to capture resources and opportunities.

One of the arguments men with chiefly ambitions put forward was that subdividing the village and creating new villages would help the locality attract more resources, since jobs and community compensation for the loss of "bush" were allocated by village. But there were also personal benefits, like those described above, for the men who became village chiefs, and it seemed that every time I returned to the oil field region there was a new village and a new chief. In the summer of 2005, the village of Ngalaba became Ngalaba 1 and Ngalaba 2. The chief of Ngalaba, who had been in the post for ten years, was able to retain 102 households in Ngalaba 1, but 123 households lined up behind the new chief in Ngalaba 2. The old chief said he had heard people in the village say they could not have an "ignorant" person—by which he meant someone who could not read or write—as chief. "In the past this wasn't important," he lamented. "What was important was the ability of the person to think." I once asked the chief of Bendoh, who was well respected among the chiefs in his canton, if he had a list of people who had lost fallowed land—land the consortium called "bush." I understood from his answer that he took my question as a critique of his performance as chief, though I had not meant it in that way. He said a local NGO had kept track of that information for them at the start of the project and that he had not kept it up out of "ignorance." He assured me that he understood the importance of keeping records, and said he was resolved to do that going forward. Village chiefs who could not read or write enlisted secretaries to perform those duties for them, and residents increasingly expected chiefs to maintain project archives. Chiefs kept lists of job seekers, records of outstanding claims, copies of complaint letters, and inventories of trees lost.

People also expected their chiefs to advocate effectively on their behalf. Residents of Ngalaba complained that the chief not only could not read or write but also could not speak French and was not an effective communicator in any language. A resident of Ngalaba 2 said that when the governor visited, the old chief asked for the intervention of the military because there was "too much disorder" in the village, and that he delivered the request while they were still standing up—a comment meant to underscore the chief's impulsiveness and lack of judgment and good manners. My informant said people were "disappointed" that the chief did not think before he spoke or examine the occasion and think about what he should say. The chiefs of the villages of canton Miandoum collectively identified three of their members to act as spokespersons in their interactions with consortium officials because, as one chief put it, they had "mastered the art of speaking in a loud voice." Administrative and diplomatic fluency—reading, writing, keeping records, speaking authoritatively, and knowing what to say for every occasion—became critical job skills for village chiefs in the time of oil.

Village chiefs triaged grievances—endorsing some, but not others; yet this was not because they internalized the consortium's policies, as the LCCs did. Like their constituents, village chiefs found the consortium's policies confusing and unfair, and they complained about them and filed grievances. One year after he took office, the new chief of Ngalaba 2 handed me a copy of his own grievance letter:

Ngalaba, August 22, 2006

Request for compensation for land:

I, [____], reclaim my land in Hollo [an area within Ngalaba] which contains 4 *karités,* of which 2 are productive and 2 *karités* that are not productive, for which we have made a claim with the local community contact for the canton whose name is [____] in 2004 that is unanswered [*sans suite*].[7]

He also handed me a list of people whose fields the consortium had occupied without paying compensation. The list was handwritten, signed, and stamped with a dye ink stamp. The list contained the names of eleven farmers, and the chief's name was first on the list.

Village chiefs had to manage the consortium's attempts to integrate them into the pipeline project by requiring them to perform the state-like function of vetting claims and selectively endorsing them, as well as the anxious and insistent demands of their constituents, who could always line up behind someone else, for effective representation and project benefits. Farmers' letters brought these competing demands and the difficulty of reconciling them to the fore. Village chiefs triaged grievance letters because the consortium's policies were enforced by a bevy of bureaucrats and a dense web of surveillance and oversight, and the chiefs worked hard to maintain their positions of authority and the advantages those positions afforded them. The attempts of local authorities to govern and to make a living from the project kept complaints in villages and domestic spaces and reformulated state power at the margins of the oil economy.

Writing Lessons

In addition to sending a copy of his letter to the LCC for the canton, Mr. Mbairo sent copies to three human rights organizations. There were a handful of human rights organizations in Chad when the pipeline project got underway. They were known mostly by their acronyms—APLFT, LTDH, and ATPDH—and their four-wheel-drive vehicles that plied the streets of N'Djamena. The pipeline project stimulated the creation of many new NGOs, including human rights groups and research and monitoring groups (*bureaux d'études*), as well as several regional networks of NGOs that described their mission as defending the rights of local populations in sites of oil exploration and production. The organizations that formed in response to the project under the broad banner of "civil society" were not all the same, but they ended up working toward the same end.

Before the World Bank approved the pipeline project in June 2000, Chadian NGOs and their international partner organizations advocated for fundamental changes to the project's design. They lobbied the World Bank to postpone the project until they had time to prepare the ground. They proposed to work with local businesses to make them more competitive for contracts, extend banking facilities to rural areas where there would be a tidal wave of cash and no easy way for people to secure or save it, and educate people about the project. The Commission Permanante de Pétrole Locale (CPPL), the umbrella group of NGOs that was headquartered in Moundou and formed to represent people affected by the Doba basin operations, argued that a delay in project implementation and a longer planning period would improve the likelihood that the project would function as a poverty reduction project. When the World Bank sidelined the CPPL's proposals and approved the project over its objections, the coalition and other civil society groups had to scramble to redefine their mission and refocus their efforts.

They took up the role of watchdog. After 2000, civil society groups directed their attention to monitoring the implementation of the project and producing (mostly denunciatory) reports on the activities of the consortium and the state. For example, they tracked how the government spent oil revenues by appointing individuals to fill the spaces reserved for "civil society" on the Collège de Contrôle et de Surveillance des Revenus Pétroliers, the World Bank–mandated body that monitors the government's use of oil revenues and supervises the bidding process for government contracts. Civil society groups also directed their attention to scrutinizing the consortium's environmental, contracting, labor, and land management practices. Members of these groups met regularly with the International Advisory Group, the External Compliance Monitoring Group, and other World Bank–sponsored monitoring bodies and even accompanied these groups on some of their missions to the oil field region. They solicited funding from international partner organizations and donor groups to collect information about the project, and they produced newsletters, reports, and websites to diffuse it, mostly to external audiences. They also used this information to file anonymous complaints on behalf of residents of the oil field region with the compliance adviser/ombudsperson at the International Finance Corporation (Groupe de Recherche Alternatives et de Monitoring du Projet Petrole Tchad-Cameroun 2011). A handful of activists became key informants for international NGOs and were regularly invited to speak about the project at global meetings and conferences.

Farmers' letters provided critical fodder for these monitoring and advocacy efforts. Most NGOs had their headquarters in N'Djamena or in regional capitals—a long way from the epicenter of project activities. Activists attached to these organizations rarely traveled to the oil field region, and when they did they often spent less than twenty-four hours before returning to the city. They therefore counted on people in the rural villages of the region to be their eyes and ears.

Early on in the pipeline project, a major activity of local NGOs was to teach people about their "rights" vis-à-vis the consortium and the state. They organized workshops and training sessions to educate farmers about the consortium's policies and Chadian law. They schooled people about land laws, regulations in the *Code de Travail* governing employment and workers' rights, and the roles of different branches of the state's security forces. They disseminated the *barème*, or the table of compensation rates the consortium had established and used in paying people for different crops and species of trees, and the definitions the consortium used to distinguish "mature" trees from "seedlings," "productive" from "nonproductive" trees, and a "field" from "bush." Civil society groups encouraged people to know their rights and to insist on them by writing letters and filing claims as part of the grievance mechanism.

People took this charge to heart. The letters showcased the extent to which residents mastered the consortium's terms, categories, and systems of classification. Letter writers quoted the compensation rates the consortium set in the *barème,* and categorized their trees according to the rubrics the consortium provided. Their letters included precise accounts of incidents and events, including dates, times, locations, and amounts. As one farmer in Ngalaba wrote:

> I have the honor of coming before you, very respectfully, to depose my grievance against Esso who destroyed my trees, including five (5) *karités,* of which three (3) were productive and two (2) nonproductive and not compensated for in the location MWIL-M5008M08 Rev1 place IN36550.[8]

Another wrote:

> I am writing to explain the problems concerning two tamarind trees, one productive and the other nonproductive, that were destroyed by Esso but they weren't paid. That day, we stopped the machine and BJ, the photographer [an Esso employee], came to take pictures of the tamarinds and he told us to let the machine work and Esso will pay and finally we have not found a good response. The taking of the land was in 2009 and the payment was the 14th of December 2009 and we started our claim in January 2010, more than 6 months ago but we haven't found a solution.

Even when the writing was halting and difficult to follow, the letters were peppered with policy talk:

> Esso has occupied with an electrical pole and wells prepared along the road to Bendoh, the side by the manifold, a line that hasn't been

paid of a length of 100m of a field the machine destroyed two productive *karités.*

I learned from letter writers that the LCCs also played an important role in shaping the form and content of their letters. When people wrote phrases or made statements that would not be accepted by the consortium, the LCCs instructed them to rewrite all or part of their letters. For example, a letter writer in Ngalaba, who was writing for his uncle who had lost land and trees without receiving a compensation payment, used the letter to educate the consortium about the region and to inform it that there was no longer any forest in canton Miandoum. He asserted that the land taken from his uncle was not "bush," as the consortium claimed, but agricultural land held fallow. The LCC told the letter writer that his categories and reasoning were *archaïque* and that these sentences needed to be struck from his letter. The LCCs dictated sentences to letter writers when their letters were not "good" until the writers learned what could—and, more important, what could not—be said. The LCCs also instructed letter writers how to address their letters. They were instructed to write to "Monsieur le chargé des dommages EEPCI a Komé Base," though no one who wrote ever learned the identity of their addressee. As a result of their interactions with NGO activists and the LCCs, farmers' letters took on a remarkable uniformity.

Beyond the instruction they received, residents of the oil field region tried to make their letters look like official documents. In so doing they participated in the mimicry the consortium initiated in asking village chiefs to stamp and sign people's grievances. Letter writers tried to give their letters weight and heft by reproducing government letterhead. They adorned their letters with symbols of the state. They wrote "Republique du Tchad" across the top of their grievances in the style of government ministries, and they copied, in longhand, the state slogan "Unité—Travail—Progrès" or "Paix—Amour—Justice," the slogan of the Mouvement Patriotique du Salut, the ruling political party. They also provided a raft of personal information about themselves, sometimes enough to fill half a page, in the style and format of national identity cards. Letter writers listed their family and given names, and where they lived, including the *sous-préfecture,* canton, and village. They gave their dates of birth and the names of their mothers and fathers. Except for the fact that they were handwritten, grievance letters looked like official documents, and they left no doubt about the identities of their authors or where to find them.

In most of the letters, people restated the consortium's policies and asked the consortium to abide by them. Their claims referenced their rights and the obligations the consortium had identified for itself and had promised to uphold. For example:

I have the respectful honor of coming before your benevolence [*sic*]
to let you know that I have a field that was used by your services as a
station for the collection of water. In doing that, they destroyed two
karités and occupied the land. And I have not come into possession of
my rights. This is why I am using this letter to ask you to enter into
my rights in terms of compensation.

As self-described watchdogs or monitors of the project, NGO activists got
tangled up in disseminating and enforcing the terms of the consortium's contractual agreements. They took a publicly critical stance toward the project and some
of the consortium's policies, but despite this they became comanagers alongside
the consortium and the World Bank. NGO activists would not recognize this
description of their work or describe the role they played in these terms. Some of
them understood farmers' grievances as a medium for the expression of "voice"
in the way A. O. Hirschman describes it—as "political action par excellence" (1970,
16). They understood the claims-making process as a way to document the effects
of the project in the oil field region and to prod the consortium to make changes
to its operational procedures in response to residents' complaints. Paradoxically,
the grievance mechanism had the opposite effect: it worked to bring public expectations into alignment with the consortium's sense of what was fair and just, and
not the other way around.

Traces

In thinking about why people wrote and why they continued to write even
after it became apparent that no response from the consortium would be forth-
coming, it was important not to dissociate the form and content of the letters from
the ways the letters circulated and how they were handled, shared, exchanged and
stored (Navaro-Yashin 2007). As I have noted above, when people made claims,
they adopted the language of the consortium and they worked to make their letters look official, even beyond acquiring the stamps and signatures the consortium
required. But it was also important to think about the letters as documents and to
follow them as tangible, material objects. Their trajectories, locations, and physical
presence (or absence) mattered, especially to their authors.

When people wrote grievance letters, they reproduced them and distributed
them widely. Mbairo sent his letter to six recipients, including the LCC for his
canton; "the base"; three human rights organizations; and himself as "the owner
of the mango tree." Letters accumulated in folders in the offices of human rights
organizations in regional towns and in the capital, but the bulk of the letters
remained in the oil field region. In some villages, the chief or his secretary kept
copies of the letters or a registry of grievances that remained open. Most of the

letters I saw were personal copies of letters kept by letter writers in their own houses. People stored their letters under mattresses or in plastic bags or suitcases along with birth certificates, national identity cards, health records, and other important documents.

While letter writers worked to archive their letters and make them public, the consortium did the opposite; it worked to expunge grievances from the official record of the project and to make it look like project implementation was proceeding smoothly. For years I tried to get information about the letters the consortium received, if not access to the letters themselves. Staff in the consortium's Socio-Economic Department and in the Public Affairs unit at Esso headquarters in N'Djamena never refused to give me the information, but they never produced it either. My quest for complaint data felt like a game in which consortium staff was constantly inventing new ways to put me off. Just before a meeting where I was supposed to be given data, the public affairs officer sent an e-mail feigning confusion about my request: "Wanted to test a couple of items with you that will allow us to do some legwork in advance from our data base. You are interested in claims that have been filed but this includes only those after the initial compensation process/land acquisition process has been completed???" Another time, after a fruitless trip to the consortium's offices, where I was supposed to pick up the claims data, the manager of the Socio-Economic Department sent a note in which he prevaricated and flat-out lied: "I apologize, I traveled to Douala but I asked H. to provide you data that she must collect from our Team in Komé. You didn't pass to collect the document, I don't know what happened. H: could you send to Lori the data you got from B. about complaints. I am sorry again." (H. never sent anything). There was always one more person I needed to see, one more set of permissions to acquire, someone who would get back to me but never did.[9]

The World Bank advises project operators to log complaints made through grievance mechanisms and to track the numbers of complaints received, resolved, unresolved, and referred to a third party. These complaints are supposed to be maintained in a database and included in the World Bank's supervision system (World Bank 2013). The consortium's first two quarterly progress reports contain the only publicly available data on the grievances people filed with the consortium. After the first two reports, the consortium dropped the section dedicated to grievances and never reinstated it. Ironically, the consortium was required to produce the quarterly progress reports under its agreement with the World Bank and as part of an effort to demonstrate transparency and accountability. This is spelled out in the standard preface that accompanies all the quarterly reports and which reads, in part,

> These reports are submitted through, and subject to verification by, the World Bank and Lender Group as a reporting requirement of the

project's partnership with the Bank and the two host countries. This report also represents a commitment to transparency by Esso and its co-venture partners. By publishing this information, the project wishes to make it possible for the World Bank and Lender Group, the citizens of the host countries, interested non-governmental organizations (NGOS) and others to stay well informed about the project as it unfolds.

A striking feature of the short-lived grievance tallies is the gap between countries. In the first quarterly report, there were "no outstanding grievances" in Chad, while in Cameroon "about 10% of registered land users" (from an unspecified number) filed complaints (EEPCI 2000). In the second report, six grievances were filed in Chad, and four of them were "closed out," while eighty-one grievances were still pending in Cameroon (EEPCI 2001). The consortium attributed the gap between countries to the implementation schedule of the project and the relative intensity of construction activities in Chad and Cameroon during these periods. But it was also the case that people in the oil field region were just finding their footing. In late 2000 and early 2001, LCCS, NGO activists, local authorities, and the residents of the cantons they served were just beginning to develop an understanding of how the project worked.

Domesticating Disputes

Wittingly or unwittingly, different kinds of intermediaries brought people's claims into alignment with the normative frame of the *Compensation and Resettlement Plan*. These actors did not always see themselves as allies of the consortium or the World Bank, yet through the grievance mechanism they were alienated from their communities and interpolated into the project as comanagers, and they assumed roles that were vital to the smooth implementation of the project. LCCS and NGO activists taught people how to write grievance letters by disseminating the consortium's policies and the terms, categories, and arguments that would make their letters legible. Village chiefs decided which claims to endorse and which to reject, and the LCCS classified people's claims as "founded" or "unfounded." These practices transformed them into middle figures and bureaucrats; they produced identification effects (Trouillot 2001). The grievance mechanism created subject populations in the oil field region that saw themselves as different from other smallholder farmers—more "modern," educated, and sophisticated—and as belonging to privileged groups or upwardly mobile classes.

These intermediaries ensured that people's grievances were framed narrowly and in direct response to the provisions of the plan. A key component of this was that letter writers had to identify as individuals who could claim exclusive rights to land, trees, crops, animals, or structures. The grievance mechanism forced letter writers to differentiate themselves from others—a dynamic Trouillot (2001), and Nicos Poulantzas (1972) before him, described as isolation effects—and to identify as private landowners even in the absence of a formal system of land titling. In fact, in 2007, the consortium began a comprehensive land mapping exercise in which all farmers had to walk the perimeters of their fields, accompanied by consortium staff with global positioning system equipment so the consortium could establish a comprehensive, geocoded database that linked individual farmers to particular plots of land and to other household members and any plots of land they claimed.

The grievance mechanism also had spatialization effects. It contained disputes in communities and families, where they would not interrupt the flow of oil. It defined and reinforced boundaries by delimiting the oil field region from the rest of the country. Within the region it kept separate domestic spaces and spaces of extraction, and it created and reified boundaries for cantons, villages, and fields. The claims-making process was choreographed to keep people away from the base camp and project operations and to maintain as much physical separation as possible between residents and extractive activities. The LCCs were middle figures in both a metaphoric and a literal sense: they alone moved between domestic spaces and spaces of extraction. To residents of the oil field region, the consortium and the World Bank remained shadowy entities for the duration of the project. The relationships between residents and consortium staff at the base camp—like the nameless and faceless *Monsieur* to whom they addressed their grievance letters—were eerily reminiscent of Franz Kafka's descriptions in *The Castle* of K's futile attempts to access the authorities who governed the village.[10] Residents' interactions with the consortium were heavily mediated, and took place through the LCCs in satellite offices and in community consultation sessions in their villages. The consortium's base camp remained a distant and mysterious world, even for people who passed by its gates every day.

The grievance mechanism provided residents of the oil field region with a language—including terms, categories, arguments, and even forms of address—for making claims that could be recognized by the consortium. In their letters, people demonstrated mastery of this new vocabulary about land and the social relations it entailed. Residents read, wrote, and recited the consortium's policies over and over again; they dictated their letters to writers, and they rewrote, copied, and recopied the texts. Compensation rates, species of trees, categories of land, and ideas about ownership became naturalized and woven into everyday interactions.

These legibility effects produced other effects. Negotiations over compensation payments often began with people who had farmed expropriated plots in the past asking the recipient of the compensation payment for "the price of the trees."

The *barème* changed people's perceptions of the relative value of different species of trees and plots, and it became possible to buy, sell, rent, pawn, and enclose land.

Trouillot did not write about state effects as taking tangible or material forms, but documents are another type of state effect. States produce documents, and letters are material traces of the state (Navaro-Yashin 2007). The letters people kept in their houses alongside other important pieces of paper function as a dispersed land registry. The letters and the claims they contain have no legal standing. Even though they approximated the form of official documents, the letters would not be accepted in a court of law or a cadastral office, and the claims made within them would not make sense to anyone outside the oil field region or the ambit of the project. But it is the physical presence of the letters—the material traces they leave in dusty files in NGO offices and especially in the villages and houses of the region—that keeps people's claims alive.

THREE

Becoming "Eligible"

At the end of a meeting at Esso's corporate headquarters in N'Djamena, where I had again failed to obtain information about grievances residents had filed with the consortium, Esso's public affairs officer presented me with a CD. At the time this felt like a consolation prize—something the public affairs officer had given me so I would not have to leave his office empty-handed. The CD contained an electronic copy of the consortium's *Environmental Management Plan* (EMP) for Chad a six-volume tome with detailed plans for waste management, compensation and resettlement, workplace health and safety, the management of oil spills, regional development, revenue management, and the construction of project facilities and infrastructure.[1]

I had not asked the public affairs officer for a copy of the EMP. Unlike the grievance letters, which the consortium guarded closely, the plan was widely available. The consortium posted the document to its website, and the World Bank distributed the EMP through its public information centers in London, Brussels, Paris, Tokyo, Washington, and N'Djamena. In Chad the consortium distributed the EMP on CD and delivered hard copies to libraries, nongovernmental organization (NGO) offices, and government offices. The EMP was also available in reading rooms the consortium had set up in the oil field region and along the route of the pipeline, ostensibly for the purpose of making project documents available to anyone who cared to view them. The hard copy versions of the EMP that I saw in libraries, offices, and reading rooms came in the form of a series of blue binders that filled entire bookshelves.

I came to understand the presence of the CD in my hand and the production and display of the blue binders as a critical part of establishing the consortium as a conscientious operator, one that adhered to global norms (Barry 2013). Whether the EMP and the other documents archived in the readings rooms were actually accessible to residents of the oil field region was not the point; in fact, I never met anyone in canton Miandoum who visited a reading room and few people in the oil field region had read any part of the EMP, which was produced in English and French and was written in dense and highly technical policy language. The point was to display the plans, to make them visible. The sheer volume of the documentation, along with the neat and coordinated appearance of the binders, conveyed to observers that the consortium's plans were detailed, comprehensive, ordered, transparent, and available.

Despite the rhetoric of corporate social responsibility and attempts like this one to make it visible through documentation, Jamie Cross (2011) has argued that standards regimes facilitate the efforts of companies to delimit their obligations and responsibilities to operators along their global supply chains. In Chad these operators included the farmers whose land the consortium needed for the project. The expropriation of their land was governed by the *Compensation and Resettlement Plan*, which comprised volume 3 of the EMP. The consortium designed the plan to adhere to the World Bank's standard on involuntary resettlement, known as Operational Directive (OD) 4.30, which states that borrowers are responsible for implementing resettlement programs that restore or improve the living standards of those who are displaced by development projects, and that displaced people should be actively involved in the design and implementation of these resettlement programs.

Resettlement and the restoration of livelihoods is a long and complicated process and has usually been carried out by nation-states in the context of infrastructure and nation-building projects like dams, power plants, or highways.[2] But private companies are increasingly implicated in resettlement schemes, including global oil companies that need access to land for their drilling and production operations. Unlike nation-states, private companies do not aim to take on complicated social rehabilitation or recovery projects with vague or open-ended timelines, and they work instead to distance and detach themselves from ongoing obligations and responsibilities to those who are displaced. These efforts to distance and detach are particularly pronounced in the case of global oil companies, whose characteristic mode of operation, as James Ferguson (2005, 2006) has shown, is to establish highly secured enclaves that are separated and cut off from the rest of the territorial nation-states in which they are located.

The distinctive features of extractive enclaves described by Ferguson were easy to recognize in the oil field region. Expatriate employees flew into and out of the region on private Dash 8s. They lived in gated and self-contained camps under conditions that contrasted sharply with those in the oil field region and had almost no contact with people in the surrounding villages[3] (Braquehais 2009; Coll 2012). But the pipeline and other project installations were not contained within these camps; they were scattered around the oil field region and were part of the everyday geography of residents' lives. In order to obtain the thousands of hectares the consortium needed for the project, it had to enter into relationships with residents that could not be limited to market exchanges and to bind itself to residents beyond the moment of the actual land transfers.

In this chapter I show how the consortium designed the *Compensation and Resettlement Plan* to minimize those commitments by distributing responsibilities for resettlement and its outcomes to other actors, and particularly to farmers themselves. I suggest that the consortium's primary objective was not to create neoliberal subjects who could remake themselves off the farm, even though it encouraged farmers to be self-sufficient and responsible and to plan, calculate, invest, and budget, and it highlighted the importance of personal characteristics like having goals, determination, commitment, and the will to succeed. The consortium was driven instead by the desire to limit its own liability for farmers' futures and to contain and curtail its involvement and investments in their recovery and rehabilitation. Devolving responsibility for resettlement and rehabilitation to farmers was a key strategy for disengagement, but this was not easy; the project of distancing and detaching entailed significant work for the consortium.

The consortium presented the *Compensation and Resettlement Plan* as a consensus document and as the product of sustained discussion and dialogue with residents. But it was difficult and time-consuming for the consortium to manage residents' anger over the loss of their land and to contain their expressions of discontent and opposition to the terms of the plan. Farmers took up responsibility for rehabilitating themselves by becoming entrepreneurial and resourceful, but in ways the consortium did not anticipate. The *Compensation and Resettlement Plan* divided people into categories—*les éligibles* and *les non-éligibles*—but the placement of people in these categories had nothing to do with the impact of the project on them. Those who became eligible for resettlement were those who acquired the skills, capacities, and savoir-faire to operate in the time of oil. In fact, farmers became so successful at becoming eligible that they created a public relations crisis that demanded the reengagement of the consortium.

The *Compensation and Resettlement Plan* signaled a mutation in the nature of involuntary resettlement. As it was carried out in the oil field region, resettlement was not a "social project" (Cernea 2008, 27) but a project based on a relational ethic of detachment, which Cross (2011) has identified as a guide to conduct and an ongoing set of performances in private sector projects. What defined resettlement in the oil field region were the efforts of the consortium to separate and detach itself from binding obligations to the farmers whose land it needed. It did this by circumscribing its obligations to those who were displaced, devolving responsibility for resettlement and rehabilitation to others, especially to farmers themselves, and ignoring resettlement programming until a crisis made this impossible.

Speaking Their Language

The consortium estimated that it would need 2,124 hectares of land in the oil field region for the project (EEPCI 1999b, vol. 3, sec. 3.2). While acknowledging that some families would be displaced, the consortium emphasized that the loss of homes and the disruption to lives would be minimized by project design, such as routing the pipeline around villages and strategically placing infrastructure on "unused" land. A condition of OD 4.30 is that affected populations be involved in the design of compensation and resettlement programs, and the consortium presented the *Compensation and Resettlement Plan* as the product of intensive community engagement and sustained discussion with residents.

It was in the course of preproject impact assessments and the community consultation sessions that formed the core of the consortium's formal consultation program that residents of the oil field region came to understand themselves as affected by the project and as eligible for particular packages of benefits. The consortium imagined the impact of the project to vary depending on how much land individual farmers, families, and communities lost to the project. The consortium defined villages as being subjected to "high," "approaching high," "moderate," or "low" impact based on the project's demands on the village land base, which shifted over time. This ranking system was used to allocate different levels of community compensation to villages.[4] Individual farmers were also defined as affected by the project to different degrees. The consortium paid compensation to farmers who lost land, but a smaller subset of those farmers, those who lost a critical proportion of their land and could no longer make a living from farming, were also supposed to become eligible for resettlement. The project divided farmers and their families into two mutually exclusive groups: *les éligibles* and *les non-éligibles*. Farmers who became "eligible" for resettlement were enrolled in consortium-sponsored training programs to learn off-farm trades or improved agricultural production methods; others did not have access to these programs. As part of the programs, farmers also gained access to benefits like agricultural credits, equipment and materials, stipends, dependent allowances, and opportunities to travel outside their villages.

Anthropologists played a vital role in both the impact assessments and the community consultation sessions. The consortium hired an American anthropologist of southern Chad, Ellen Patterson Brown, to interface with local communities. Brown's counterpart in the rain forest region of Cameroon was Jean-Félix Luong, an emeritus professor of anthropology at the University of Yaoundé. According to the consortium's website, Luong had "studied the Bagyeli/Bakola people of Cameroon for decades," just as Brown had worked for decades in southern Chad, first as a Peace Corps volunteer and later as a professional anthropologist and development consultant for USAID, CARE, and other aid organizations (EEPCI 1999a; Mallaby 2004). The consortium described the anthropologists' knowledge of the region and their fluency in local languages as assets that could help with the development of compensation and resettlement programs that were sensitive to "local African cultural values" (EEPCI 1999b, vol. 3, sec. 1.7.3).

In the years leading up to the project, Brown and her Chadian assistants gathered information about the oil field region—including its geography, patterns of land use, social organization, housing, education, health, people's access to media, and commerce—as well as the possible impacts of the project on local communities and methods of mitigating those impacts (Dames and Moore 1997). They held public consultation sessions with residents, reviewed public records, organized focus groups, and conducted interviews and household surveys. The preproject field research and impact assessments were conducted in hundreds of villages along the proposed route of the pipeline, but they centered on the villages of the oil field region, where the need for land was most heavily concentrated. Public consultation continued throughout the project period. Villages in canton Miandoum were repeatedly visited by Brown and the local community contacts (LCCs), who provided information about how the compensation and resettlement scheme operated, what the consortium would pay for crops and trees, under what conditions payments would be made, and who would be eligible for resettlement benefits. Between 1993 and 2003, the consortium reported holding nearly 5,500 consultation sessions, which it claimed constituted "one of the most extensive public consultation efforts for a single project in the history of Africa" (Exxon-Mobil, n.d.).

The consortium described the community consultation sessions as venues for open and freewheeling exchanges that lasted "four to five hours" and were brought to an end "by the people attending, when they felt they had adequately expressed their ideas and opinions" (EEPCI 1999b, vol. 3, sec. 2.2.7). The consortium emphasized that the meetings were "not Question and Answer sessions" and that people could bring up any topic they wanted to discuss. They noted that "all groups, including less vocal groups, not just the local power structure, had many opportunities to ask questions and state their ideas." Since Brown and her assistants spoke the local language, the consortium claimed that they "captured for the record most nuances, contentious issues, and informal comments, as well as commendations and recommendations."

By the consortium's account, the meetings were occasions during which residents could express their demands, desires, and preferences and hash out the terms of land transfers and their own compensation and resettlement. The consortium might have authored the plan, but the shape and content of the compensation and resettlement programs reflected a consensus view generated by communities themselves in consultation with a cultural anthropologist who spent time in their villages, spoke their language, and was sensitive to local ways of doing things. The programs were the products of a process that mimicked the local political process, and they reflected a thorough vetting of ideas and the outcome of exhaustive and inclusive deliberations: "Discussion and reflection in small groups are a fundamental element in the local political system. Consensus and public support are developed through this process. Thus traditional political processes generated the conclusions and recommendations shaped over the course of these meetings and contained in this Plan" (EEPCI 1999b, vol. 3, sec. 2.2.7).

Dissension was difficult to locate in project texts, but it was not difficult to spot on the ground. The modalities the consortium used to engage residents and the ways the consortium described them obscured the divergent interests of the consortium and residents as well as the tensions and conflicts between them. During the impact assessment process, Brown became well known to people in canton Miandoum, who referred to her (not kindly) as the *tête pensante*—the "mastermind"—behind the consortium's land expropriation scheme. In canton Miandoum, people rejected the claims of the consortium, the World Bank, and the Chadian government that their land "belong[ed] to the state" (Guyer 2002, 113) and that they should receive compensation for their labor on the land but not for the land itself. They contested the consortium's understandings of local systems of land tenure and the division of their land into "fields" (land that was under cultivation) and "bush" (land that lay fallow and was therefore, according to the consortium, collectively owned or part of the village land base). They also challenged the ahistorical manner in which compensation and resettlement benefits were awarded to the person working the field at the time of expropriation without consideration of who had used the field in the past, and registered complaints about the types of training programs the consortium sponsored, the duration of the programs, the quality and types of material support the consortium provided after training, and many other provisions of the programs.

Residents of the canton found the community consultation sessions alienating and frustrating. Many people stopped attending the sessions; others came only to listen and to collect information but not to participate. The mood at many of the sessions was argumentative and confrontational; they sometimes devolved into shouting matches between angry farmers and the LCCs, who worried about their security at these events and refused to attend the sessions alone. People complained that Brown and her assistants came to the sessions accompanied by military police and by local authorities, who chastised them for making demands on the consortium and accused them of complaining about the project to NGOs and human rights activists. In response to a complaint filed by local NGOs about the consortium's use of military police in the consultation sessions, the consortium wrote the following:

Gendarme Support and Interaction

Issue: A problem identified in Chad by NGOs and the public during consultation related to the presence of gendarmes during the consultation process. The people did not always feel comfortable expressing themselves freely in the presence of armed gendarmes. The gendarmes were not always sensitive to the nature of the process, and it was felt they might have been a hindrance to the communications being encouraged.

Action: Because of the political insecurity in this region of Chad, particularly in the earlier years of the project, it was deemed important to have gendarmes on duty during the consultation process. However, in a multi-step process to address this concern and encourage open two-way communications during consultation, gendarmes were first counseled about the process and about the conduct expected of them during the process. A second step reduced the number of gendarmes present during consultation meetings. And, finally, the number of gendarmes have been reduced to zero during consultation; their services are utilized only as reconnaissance prior to each meeting. (EEPCI 1999a, sec. 9.34)

This statement is taken from a document the consortium produced to demonstrate its responsiveness to feedback it received during a public comment period about the proposed design of the project. The text included a series of "issues" identified by NGOs or "the public" and a series of "actions" the consortium took in response to the issues raised. The point of the section on "Gendarme Support and Interaction" was not to assess how communications might have been shaped or compromised by the presence of armed gendarmes or by the practice of using them to conduct reconnaissance prior to each meeting. The consortium never questioned the reliability of the information produced in the community consultation sessions, where "people did not always feel comfortable expressing themselves freely"; nor did it consider the possible implications of the NGOs' claims for any decisions that were taken. Instead, the consortium's aim in producing the document was to demonstrate its own responsiveness to problems NGOs identified and its fidelity to a standards regime that required the consortium to elicit community participation and feedback.

As this excerpt demonstrates, tension, friction, and conflict over the project—glossed in the consortium's response as "political insecurity"—structured the consultation process. The consortium emphasized that consultation was widespread and comprehensive because Brown and her assistants "t[ook] consultation to the people" rather than holding centralized hearings in towns (EEPCI 1999a, sec. 9.5). The consortium presented the thousands of decentralized consultation sessions as a way of dealing with the ethnic and cultural diversity of the area covered by the project (even though ethnic and cultural diversity on the Chad side of the project was limited) and as a means of consulting people without imposing travel burdens on them.[5] In the context of the Baku-Tbilisi-Ceyhan (BTC) pipeline project,

Andrew Barry (2013) has suggested that oil companies targeted consultation to certain villages to avoid raising expectations in communities not defined as affected. While these considerations may have played a role in structuring the formal consultation program in Chad, it was also the case that the small, informal gatherings that were organized, one village at a time, allowed the consortium to minimize crowds, manage and contain the anger and dissent expressed at these events, and prevent disaffection from escalating and spiraling out of control.

Conflict and tension over the project were scrubbed from the record in other ways, too. During the public comment period, the consortium reported receiving over nine thousand comments from people in Chad and Cameroon and described the analysis of this feedback as part of an "adaptive design" process that led to "hundreds of project changes" (EEPCI 1999a, sec. 9.1). Twenty-one percent of the comments came from the public consultation sessions, but most of the comments the consortium received—64 percent—came from the reading rooms, where visitors could leave notes or requests in a log. The consortium submitted the comments it received to "statistical analysis" and reported that this analysis revealed fifteen general categories of response (EEPCI 1999a, sec. 9.9). The largest category of response was "positive views on the project" (22 percent), followed by "hiring/job opportunities/employment/training" (19 percent), and "compensation/resettlement" (12 percent; EEPCI 1999a, sec. 9.9). By presenting the analysis of public feedback as a technical and analytical exercise driven by objective and dispassionate statistical methods, the consortium was able to tame expressions of anger, opposition, and anxiety over the project. It was also able to repackage public comments under a series of innocuous headings, such as "project funding/Bank's role," "socioeconomics/cultural," "environmental documents," and "general project/technical/schedule," or headings that emphasized potential project benefits, such as "hiring/job opportunities/employment/training" or "roads/construction/infrastructure." The consortium was able to sideline some comments as having "no direct relation to the project" and to craft categories in ways that suggested certain types of project changes but not others.

Documents, blue binders, reading rooms, and CDs designated the oil field region as a space of transnational governance based on standards. These spaces were created by the production and dissemination of information about the project and not by erecting physical enclaves of the type Ferguson (2005, 2006) has described (Barry 2013). But the consortium's formal consultation program, the LCCS, and the preproject fieldwork and impact assessments conducted by Brown and her assistants also did this work. People learned through these channels that some individuals, families, and communities were more affected by the project than others, and that some were eligible for benefits and services, such as resettlement, while others were not. The consultation program created identifications and expectations among residents of the oil field region, but this process was not smooth or consensual.

The consortium's claims to knowledge about local culture and social organization and to privileged, insider access to this knowledge obscured intense contestation over the expropriation of land and the terms of the compensation and resettlement programs. The consortium published photographs of Brown sitting cross-legged on the ground next to villagers or on her hands and knees, drawing in the dirt, as evidence of a participatory, engaged, and culturally sensitive process of elaborating the compensation and resettlement programs.[6] In contrast, the picture that emerged on the ground was one in which the interests of residents and the consortium were so divergent and tensions were so high that consultation had to be carefully stage-managed. The consortium distanced itself from local communities and worked to collect their responses in "low-touch" ways—by culling anonymous feedback from logs in reading rooms that were far from the site of the project and from the secondhand reports of embedded (and embattled) LCCs. Statistical operations confined the emotions conveyed via written comments to innocuous categories. Community consultation sessions were more difficult to manage and had to be handled one community at a time, and even then the sessions could only be carried out under the constant and visible threat of force.

Do-It-Yourself Resettlement

The conclusions the consortium drew from Brown's fieldwork distributed responsibility for involuntary resettlement and its outcomes across a network of actors. This network included NGOs that were supposed to design and conduct the training of displaced farmers and advise them about their resettlement options as well as local authorities in host communities who were supposed to receive displaced farmers and provide them with replacement land. But responsibilities for rehabilitation and recovery fell particularly heavily on the farmers themselves.

One of the conclusions the consortium drew from Brown's fieldwork was that resettlement was a naturally occurring phenomenon in the oil field region; it argued that Brown's data showed that people left their villages to establish splinter villages, and that they moved frequently from one location to another, though usually within the same canton. The consortium claimed that people relocated for a variety of reasons, including lack of fertile land, illness, and marriage but also "sibling rivalry," "poor social skills," and "new adventure" (EEPCI 1999b, vol. 3, sec. 2.3.1). According to the *Compensation and Resettlement Plan*, the movement of individuals and family groups was so much a part of everyday life that "resettlement does not pose any new issue which the culture has not already resolved" (EEPCI 1999b, vol. 3, sec. 2.3.4). As a result, the consortium determined that people affected by the project should be left to move themselves or to self-resettle.

By the consortium's account, resettlement was not a process the state, the consortium, or some other agency had to—or even should—engineer; interfering with a process that was deemed to be so natural would make resettlement cumbersome and inefficient, and would only impede and complicate a process that people could best manage themselves:

> Resettlement under this Plan will take advantage of the common experience of self-resettlement so typical of the area. The choice of where to resettle is left to the individual or household, and adequate time will be allowed for the decision.
>
> EEPCI [Esso Exploration and Production Chad, Inc.] and TOTCO [Tchad Oil Transportation Company] will not decide on the place where people will resettle. Instead, the resettlers themselves will access land in the traditional way and on traditional and customary terms. Not only does this replicate the cultural pattern, but experience from other resettlement projects has shown a higher success rate when resettlers and local authorities carry out negotiations among themselves, without government or agency interference. If difficulty is encountered in finding a new piece of land, the EDR [Esso Designated Representative] may act as a facilitator. If necessary, the next higher level of local authorities will be asked to broker an agreement. (EEPCI 1999b, vol. 3, sec. 6.5)[7]

By producing, with the help of a cultural anthropologist, this picture of a highly mobile and self-regulating population, the consortium could depict the process of evacuating people from the scene and taking their land as natural and even helpful, since those who self-resettled received compensation as well as "decision-making facilitation" and "assistance with logistics" from the consortium (EEPCI 1999b, vol. 3, sec. 6.5). The pipeline and industrial oil production could be slipped into a local ecology where people were in the habit of moving and therefore could have neither deep attachments to the land required for the project nor the need for much assistance once they were forced to leave it.

Farmers who opted not to self-resettle could choose to enroll in a consortium-sponsored training program to replace lost income from farming. The programs were offered through local NGOs and included programs in off-farm trades such as carpentry, welding, masonry, tailoring, restaurant operation, and motorcycle repair. Alternatively, farmers could enroll in a training program in improved agricultural production methods that was supposed to help them use their remaining landholdings more intensively. Extension agents attached to local NGOs taught farmers techniques like composting, "weeding on time," "planting on time," thinning plants, and planting in rows. They also taught farmers how to grow cash crops like onions, and how to transform agricultural products into marketable commodities like soap and wine.

The consortium said that Brown's fieldwork showed that residents of the oil field region had already begun to diversify their income sources in response to land pressure. The training programs were supposed to support farmers in the use of coping mechanisms they had already adopted, and they constituted alternatives to resettlement that farmers themselves had proposed in the course of the community consultation sessions:

> In recent decades, local people have been dealing with problems related to the availability of productive land, increasing pressure on available land, and soil infertility by using less traditional means. The latter include raising soil fertility with farm equipment and inputs, and growing valuable cash crops for money to buy food. Others earn off-farm income to buy food.
>
> In line with these efforts, the Plan will advise people eligible for resettlement about two alternatives they may consider making resettlement a last recourse. . . .
>
> Local people proposed these two alternatives as reasonable and desirable alternatives to resettlement that would help them compensate for the lost production and income on their lost field labor and crops. (EEPCI 1999b, vol. 3, sec. 6.3)

The training programs lasted no more than one year or one agricultural cycle, and most of the off-farm programs lasted a significantly shorter time. Farmers who participated in the training programs had to demonstrate that they were worth the continued investment of the consortium's resources if they wanted to remain eligible for ongoing training and support. They had to show they had been "assiduous in applying their training" to receive more of it (EEPCI 2013, 24). One of the farmers I followed left his sewing machine set up under a hangar in his concession in the event consortium staff made a monitoring visit. He complained that there was no tailoring work in the village and that he could have made more money by renting the machine to a tailor in town, but then he would jeopardize his eligibility for future trainings that were floated as possibilities to farmers but were not programmed or guaranteed as part of the resettlement process.

Consortium staff determined whether eligible farmers merited additional support on a case-by-case basis; their decisions were based on criteria such as whether trainees "take ownership of their own recovery process," "have the will to move forward," and "demonstrate that they are able and willing to make a tangible contribution in terms of time, effort, energy, and even assets in order to achieve what must be his [*sic*] goal" (EEPCI 2013, 24). Those who were not sufficiently committed to these goals—as evidenced, for example, by selling materials or inputs the consortium provided or showing no signs of practicing their trade during routine monitoring visits—became ineligible for additional resources and support (ECMG 2012). The consortium placed strict limits on its commitments to farmers and reserved the option to withdraw from efforts to rehabilitate farmers at any time. Even in the case of farmers who met the consortium's ambiguous standards, the consortium described the role it would take as "a support role rather than a leadership role" (EEPCI 2013, 24).

The training programs were not attempts to mold farmers according to neoliberal logics so much as they were efforts to delimit the consortium's obligations to farmers who had been displaced. The consortium's demands that farmers demonstrate self-sufficiency and "the will to move forward," even by using their own assets to do so, contrast sharply with most existing descriptions of involuntary resettlement programs. Michael Cernea, one of the chief architects of the World Bank's policies on involuntary resettlement and one of the most prolific writers on the subject, has described resettlement as a "project within a project" (2008, 26). In dozens of publications that span more than three decades, Cernea argues that involuntary resettlement projects need to be thought of as complex and comprehensive social engineering efforts embedded in technical and infrastructure projects like the pipeline project. His vision of resettlement is a product of the development era, but it continues to shape an impressive body of work on involuntary resettlement in the post-development period:

> On one side, we have a vast engineering endeavor built around technological objectives; on the other side, a social project completely knotted around socio-economic, cultural, relief, and development objectives, to be implemented while facing a displacement-resistant and risk-averse population. The "component" [the resettlement project] is tasked with a truly extraordinary burden—to construct a new productive basis, new habitat, new social services networks, new livelihoods for large groups—yet is not given full-fledged project means to do all this. (Cernea 2008, 27)

Resettlement in the oil field region was not the kind of "social project" Cernea has described. The consortium did not take up the task of "construct[ing] a new productive basis, new habitat, new social services networks, new livelihoods for large groups." In fact, few families moved (the exact number is hard to pinpoint, but it was probably fewer than fifty), and those that did managed the relocation chiefly on their own. The consortium used Brown's fieldwork to argue that the resettlement program and the options available to farmers reflected local ways of life and the habits, preferences, and trajectories of people in the oil field region. It suggested that it did not need to—and in fact should not—resettle farmers, because they successfully resettled themselves all the time. Those who wanted an alternative to self-resettlement received exactly what they asked for: training in a trade or in improved agricultural production methods and support for income diversification strategies they had already begun to explore as part of adapting to land shortages. But the consortium was not tasked with the "burden" of ensuring that the programs led to employment or provided farmers with replacement income; the responsibility for finding jobs, or converting training into a livelihood or a supplemental income stream, or even of remaining eligible for additional training, fell to the residents themselves.

The consortium underscored that the role of its socioeconomic team in the resettlement process was to facilitate and advise—to offer choices, but not to make them for farmers. Consortium staff provided general information about the advantages and disadvantages of different training programs; they helped farmers assess their aptitudes for certain trades and the markets in their villages for specific types of skills and services. But it was up to farmers to select from several resettlement options the ones best suited to their skills, talents, and future possibilities and to make those choices work. While consortium staff helped orient farmers, the farmers themselves were responsible for the outcomes of their decisions and actions, and this was clearly articulated in the plan:

> EEPCI and/or TOTCO recognizes that it will be difficult for individuals and households to choose between alternatives because of their long-term impacts on the economic viability of the household. To assist individuals, households and communities in making informed decisions concerning compensation and resettlement options, EEPCI and/or TOTCO will designate a representative, or EDR, who will be the facilitator to:
>
> • Help people and their villages understand and analyze the individual's situation, capacities, economic circumstances, and future before endorsing a final compensation choice,
>
> • Provide as much opportunity as possible for individuals and households to make a wise decision among the various compensation and resettlement alternatives available, and
>
> • Work with the affected parties during the construction period to implement their choices.
>
> In the end, the decision is that of the individual. EEPCI and/or TOTCO cannot be responsible for varying outcomes. (EEPCI 1999b, vol. 3, sec. 6.3)

The consortium responded to resettlement failures in ways that underscored its nonbinding attachments to residents. When the resettlement programs were shown to be ineffective in helping farmers make up for the loss of their land, the consortium introduced an "improved consultation process" that reinforced its own detached position (Barclay and Koppert 2007). The process, called the Five Steps of Reflection, required farmers to participate in a protracted period of reflection before selecting a resettlement option. Farmers had to be counseled by their peers, village chiefs, village elders, their entire communities, and members of the consortium's socioeconomic team before they could make a final decision about a resettlement option. In describing this "improved" process, the consortium claimed that it "ensures that eligible farmers get the information and time that they need to understand their options and make the right choice for them" (EEPCI 2011, 46). The failure of the resettlement programs was not an occasion for the consortium to modify or improve the programs—to "construct . . . new livelihoods for large groups" or to assume "a truly extraordinary burden" (Cernea 2008, 27). It was an occasion to remind residents of the limits of the consortium's liability for their futures.

In fact, responsibility for the failure of the resettlement programs was consistently pinned on farmers. If the training programs failed to restore farmers' incomes, the consortium asserted, it was because they did not take time to think ahead, reflect, or make informed choices; it was because they did not work hard enough or have goals, or because they were poor managers of resources and money. Evaluation teams and the World Bank's monitoring groups reproduced these ideas,[8] but on occasion they also admonished the consortium for its own lack of involvement in the postcompensation process and for the way its agents addressed farmers. For example, the ECMG wrote:

> Scolding beneficiaries of individual compensation because some of them did not use compensation well or are alcoholic is inappropriate. Though it would have been a good practice to set up an advisory system at the start of the Project to help people, if they so wished, on how to invest their compensation (and this was not implemented), local people are right when they say the money they received for compensation is their own and they can do whatever they want with it. (ECMG 2012, 69)

As Catherine Dolan and Mary Johnstone-Louis (2011) point out in their study of South African Avon entrepreneurs, devolving corporate social responsibility to the poor makes it possible to attribute programmatic failures to individual flaws because people can never have "enough" motivation, drive, or commitment.

Becoming "Eligible"

For the residents of canton Miandoum, the categories of *éligible* and *non-éligible* came to distinguish those who were quick-witted, enterprising, and able to derive certain benefits from the project from those who did not share these characteristics and capacities. To be *un éligible* was not a neutral descriptor; people used the term to describe friends, neighbors, and family members, or to identify a person to a stranger, and one's status as *un éligible* was one of the first attributes residents of the oil field region mentioned when speaking about another. The response to a question about the identity of a groom, or a party to a land deal, or the person on the back of the motorcycle that just passed by might begin with the statement, "C'est un eligible." This statement conveyed a lot. People understood by it that the person in question was sharp, savvy, and clever—a person who knew how to operate in the time of oil, a person who could size up opportunities and position himself to capture benefits from the project. People admired *les éligibles,* and were both pleased about and envious of their success.

People also talked about *les non-éligibles*—and especially the farmers who tried to become eligible or who had the opportunity to do so but failed. I once saw a group of young men hoot with laughter as they took turns mimicking the older men in their village who had been slow to catch on and who had boasted to the consortium's agents about the vast tracts of land their ancestors cleared, completely oblivious to the fact that they were simultaneously dashing their chances of winning resettlement benefits. The implication was that these men were too set in their ways and lacked the ingenuity and the flexibility of mind to recognize that wealth in land, an asset and a source of pride in the past, was a liability in the instant of responding to the consortium's agents.

The categories of *éligible* and *non-éligible* distinguished people who could access land from those who could not. It became difficult for some people, including women (as I will show in chapter 4), to access land once the consortium attached monetary values to crops and especially to trees. But the categories of *éligible* and *non-éligible* also distinguished those who learned what to say once they had successfully staked a claim to land and transformed it into a "field" from those who did not. How to answer questions about landholdings and family size was a frequent topic of conversation in the early years of the project. The consortium used a formula to determine farmers' eligibility for resettlement, which was included in the *Compensation and Resettlement Plan.*[9] But farmers did not have access to the plan, and they never knew with any precision how the consortium chose to place them in one or the other category. This information was also not shared in the community consultation sessions, so people had to learn how to become eligible in other ways.

Their struggles about what to say to the consortium's agents were not about truth-telling in any straightforward sense, though they were interpreted as such by the consortium. While everyone wanted to become eligible for resettlement (though no one wanted to become land poor), there were also many ways farmers could respond to these questions and could represent their families and their land-holdings to the consortium's agents. Take the case of Bessandji, whose family I followed. When Bessandji's father died in the early 1990s, Bessandji, his mother, and his four brothers inherited his land. Bessandji's paternal relatives had claims to the land since a common ancestor had initially cleared it, just as Bessandji had claims to the land they farmed even if he had never exercised them. Bessandji and his extended family did not formally divide up the land or claim exclusive rights to particular fields; they settled into certain patterns of land use, but these were flexible and they were renegotiated as plots were fallowed and as family members moved, died, married and had children who also needed land to farm. How, then, should Bessandji account to the consortium for his land and his family? What land should he count? Which sets of relations should figure in his claims?

Farmers quickly learned how the compensation scheme worked. They swapped compensation stories, studied their compensation papers with the help of those who had been to school, and memorized the rates attached to different kinds of crops and species of trees. But what it took to become eligible for re-settlement benefits was a more elusive piece of information. Some people learned faster than others that it was advantageous to represent themselves as land poor to the consortium's agents. Eventually, however, most people learned what to say; in fact, they became so successful at mastering eligibility for resettlement that it created a public relations crisis.

Two Reports

In March 2007, a piece by Lesley Wroughton, a correspondent for Reuters, ran in major international newspapers under the headline "World Bank Tells Exxon to Fix Chad Compensation" (Wroughton 2007). The piece set off a flurry of e-mails inside the World Bank, including a memo from a spokesperson for the bank's International Finance Corporation (IFC) that suggested that he and other World Bank officials had succeeded in shaping the storyline of the piece in their interviews with Wroughton: "The story is in line with what we had aimed for: World Bank/IFC pushes Exxon to do the right thing and Exxon has agreed to do so." The e-mails that bank staff circulated about the memo and Wroughton's piece contained jokes, banter about current events in their different locations around the world, and personal notes about plans for leaving work early. Their commentary and the breeziness of their correspondence made it clear that they had averted a full-blown public relations crisis, or at least had inoculated themselves and the consortium as best they could.

The publication of Wroughton's story was prompted by the release of a report, authored by consultants Robert Barclay and George Koppert and commissioned by ExxonMobil as part of its agreement with the World Bank, on the first major evaluation of the consortium's compensation and resettlement program. The *Barclay-Koppert Report* said that the consortium had taken far more land in the oil field region than anyone had anticipated and that the continued expansion of the project and the incremental and ongoing expropriations were jeopardizing the livelihoods of local residents and contributing to a crisis of social reproduction. The figures were staggering. By the end of 2006, twelve thousand people and 1,640 households had been affected by the project. But what was most alarming was how much land affected families had lost. About 60 percent had lost more than 20 percent of their land; half had lost more than 50 percent. More than 900 households had been "seriously affected" by the project—many times more than the consortium's initial estimate of 60 to 150 households.

The report was released just as the consortium was about to embark on a major expansion of project infrastructure and another round of expropriation, and it raised serious doubts about the long-term viability of the villages and families at the epicenter of the project. Barclay and Koppert recommended a major restructuring of the compensation and resettlement program; they recommended changes in project design to reduce the number of fields that were fragmented or divided into unusable bits by project infrastructure, and a significant expansion of the training programs in improved agricultural production methods to give farmers time to adopt more intensive farming techniques. They also encouraged the consortium to identify replacement land for families that had been made land poor, and to consider providing compensation to those families in the form of "land for land" (Barclay and Koppert 2007, sec. 8.7).

Within weeks of the publication of Wroughton's piece, the consortium responded to the *Barclay-Koppert Report* by announcing a sweeping set of reforms known as the *Land Use Mitigation Action Plan,* or *LUMAP.* One aim of the *LUMAP* was to develop a comprehensive land use map so that changes in access to land could be monitored in real time and remedial actions could be taken before families became nonviable. Another was to collect information about farmers' land assets that the consortium could use in the place of farmers' self-reports. Beginning with the most severely affected villages, consortium staff went door to door to conduct a population census and to map farmers' landholdings using global positioning system technology; they transported farmers from their villages to their fields and asked them to walk the perimeters of their plots. The consortium used this information to create a relational database that linked individual farmers with houses, other family members, and specific, geocoded plots of land. They developed a "color-coded flagging system" to track the level of project impact on villages (EEPCI 2008c) and to classify households as "wealthy," "comfortable," "marginal," or "non-viable" based on the extent of their landholdings (EEPCI 2013).

Two years after the release of the *Barclay-Koppert Report,* the consortium presented the initial results of this land mapping exercise, which had been completed in the most severely affected villages and was being extended to others. By the consortium's account, the LUMAP exercises revealed that only 15 percent of the nearly nine hundred households classified as "severely affected" in the consortium's proprietary compensation database and in the *Barclay-Koppert Report* were "truly eligible" for resettlement (EEPCI 2009, 10). Most of the people who had participated in the consortium's training programs did not qualify for resettlement benefits. The consortium offered a table to illustrate the lack of consistency in farmers' self-reports about their families and especially their landholdings over time and to suggest that the information in their proprietary database was unreliable. The table shows "land takes" for one farmer who lost a fraction of a *corde* of land in each of seven successive expropriations carried out between 2001 and 2007 (see table 3.1).[10] According to the consortium's records, the farmer lost just over two *cordes* of land in total, yet the farmer's reports of his land reserves (in the column labeled "Corde") bear little relation to the consortium's record of its cumulative impact on him over the life of the project.

In the space of two years, the consortium produced two diametrically opposed accounts of the effects of the compensation and resettlement programs on residents of the oil field region. It concluded that the account based on the LUMAP exercises was more accurate than the account based on farmers' self-reports and the compensation database. The consortium read the reports as methodological exercises that produced more or less objective or accurate estimates of the numbers of farmers made land poor by the project. But these representations might be read instead as contingent products of the consortium's policies and the strategic calculations of farmers who were learning how to become eligible for project benefits and responding to demands to become resourceful and self-sufficient.

Until 2007 and the start of the LUMAP exercises, the consortium relied entirely on farmers' self-reports about their families and landholdings to categorize them as *éligible* or *non-éligible* (Barclay and Koppert 2007, sec. 6.7). As the reports and the Reuters article showed, the consortium did not update farmers' dossiers or use these records to monitor the impact of the project on families. Barclay and Koppert's findings were based on information in the consortium's database, and so was the "faulty" data the consortium presented in the table from the LUMAP report

Table 3.1. Chronological land take of an individual

Date	Dependent	Corde	Exact Land Take (Corde)	Cumulative Land Take
10/18/2001	6	21	0.301	0.301
4/11/2005	6	3	0.216	0.517
5/9/2005	5	8	0.816	1.333
9/26/2005	6	3	0.052	1.385
9/26/2005	6	3	0.026	1.411
10/3/2005	6	3	0.262	1.673
3/12/2007	10	1	0.521	2.194

This table demonstrates how the declarative data reliability (for Dependent and Corde) is less than adequate. As presented, answers are not consistent over time. In this example, the individual started with 21 *cordes* for 6 dependents. Six years later, after a cumulative land take of 2.1 *cordes*, he declares that he has land use of only 1 *corde* (EEPCI 2008b, 4).

(see table 3.1). The consortium's failure to track the impact of land loss on farmers and their families could be read as incompetence, a case of sloppy record keeping. Barclay and Koppert pointed out that the compensation database was poorly designed and was riddled with errors and inconsistencies. No standard units were used to record the amount of land expropriated or retained, and farmers had multiple dossiers because their names were spelled differently by different land transfer agents. The impact of land loss on families could not be assessed or monitored because the dossiers of individual family members could not be linked to look at household-level effects.

But the disarray of the database revealed something more than just ineptitude, disinterest, or indifference. It revealed that becoming eligible for resettlement was a form of training. Farmers learned how to become eligible over time and over multiple rounds of expropriation; those who were classified as *non-éligible* could keep trying to become *éligible* by accessing and clearing land, and by searching out more and better information about how resettlement worked. In order to become eligible for the training programs, farmers had to demonstrate that they were industrious, calculating, motivated, competitive, and discerning consumers of information. This is similar to the circular paradox of reflexive government Mitchell Dean (1999) describes in that these are exactly the skills and attributes the training programs were supposed to inculcate as they prepared farmers to function as small business owners and agricultural entrepreneurs. Demonstrating entrepreneurialism was a precondition of entering a training program where those skills were taught, and becoming eligible for resettlement was itself a kind of training that molded farmers and helped them develop the characteristics and capacities needed to succeed in a more market-based economy.

This is evident from two seemingly anomalous findings in the report that Barclay and Koppert never draw together nor juxtapose. On the one hand, the training programs were wildly unsuccessful; few people who attended them were able to transition to off-farm employment, even on a part-time basis. Farming remained the primary source of income for all farmers who opted to learn a trade. Barclay and Koppert estimated that 87 percent of the farmers trained in a trade never—or seldom—used their training, and that only farmers who had practiced a trade before they enrolled in the training programs were able to use their skills more frequently (Barclay and Koppert 2007, sec. 5.3). The revenue that farmers generated from practicing a trade was less than 10 percent of what would have been needed to offset the loss of land, and it was not sufficient to restore farmers' incomes to preproject levels (2007, sec. 5.2). The results were no better for farmers who participated in the improved agricultural production programs. The director of those programs told Barclay and Koppert that participants increased their yields by 10 to 20 percent, but this was only enough to offset the loss of a small amount of land (2007, sec. 6.2). In short, the training programs impoverished farmers and their families; they did not make up for the loss of land.

On the other hand, in a different section of their report Barclay and Koppert concluded that the more households were affected by the project, the better off they were. Households that lost no land to the project, and therefore never received compensation or resettlement benefits, registered the lowest standard of living. Households that were "lightly or moderately" affected by the project fared somewhat better. But households that were "seriously affected" by the project and had, in principle, become land poor as a result of repeated expropriations registered the highest on a standard of living index. Barclay and Koppert, and the consortium after them, took these findings as evidence that the compensation and resettlement programs "worked." Yet, the *Barclay-Koppert Report* never asked how it was that farmers who participated in training programs that failed to offset their losses or restore their incomes to preproject levels could be better off than their counterparts who never lost land in the first place or who lost land but did not become eligible for resettlement benefits.

The compensation and resettlement programs created a new category of persons who came out on top *despite* the training programs and not because of them. Farmers assumed the burdens and responsibilities for rehabilitating themselves because they had to, and because the consortium distanced and detached itself or withdrew from these activities as quickly as possible. This meant retraining themselves, but first it meant becoming eligible for the opportunity to retrain themselves or to acquire ancillary resources and privileges by showing the consortium they were industrious, ingenious, and committed to their own recovery.

Fingerprints

Descriptions of mutations in the construction of involuntary resettlement, as distinct from shifts in resettlement policy,[11] are absent from the writing on involuntary resettlement. This absence is especially curious given the attention paid to mutations in development, and claims by Cernea and others that resettlement projects are development projects. Clues that a mutation is under way emerge from surveying the language used to describe resettlement in the oil field region. In project documents, resettlement is associated with a cluster of terms that includes "choice," "options," "responsibility," "entrepreneurial," and "self-resettlement." Absent from this cluster are terms like "social," "project," "relief," and "development"— the language of Cernea's "project within a project." Cris Shore and Susan Wright (1997) suggest that semantic shifts in key words are signs of a struggle to formulate a new discourse and to give it institutional authority, and that these shifts are the equivalent of "fingerprints" that can be used to trace more profound transformations in rationalities of governance. The material presented in this chapter is an attempt to follow some of those clues beyond their documentary sources and to examine how the underlying logic operates in the practices of large, private oil companies.

The consortium's adherence to global standards took visible and material form in the *Compensation and Resettlement Plan* and in the reading rooms, blue binders, and CDs. These material artifacts of the project communicated the message— even to those who could not read—that the consortium adhered to ethical principles in displacing families and communities. But the content of the plans inside those binders also mattered.

The consortium did not make resettlement benefits broadly available in the oil field region. Not everyone in canton Miandoum became eligible for resettlement, even though everyone was touched by the project. The consortium defined villages, families, and individuals as more or less affected by the project, delimiting its obligations, and created identifications and expectations around those categories. People came to identify as "project affected" and as having certain rights through the consortium's public consultation program. As the consortium's staff anthropologist, Brown produced knowledge about local communities, but she also shared information with those communities about themselves and the project. Conflicts and tensions over the expropriation of land structured the public consultation program and the modalities the consortium used to interact with residents and elicit their feedback in ways that highlighted and deepened the consortium's distance and detachment from local communities.

To become eligible for resettlement benefits, people in canton Miandoum had to show themselves to be self-starters who were hardworking, shrewd, and calculating before they could become eligible for the training programs that were supposed to inculcate precisely those skills and attributes. Hence the paradox that the training programs were not successful, but the people who attended them were. Farmers were cut off from additional training and support if they failed to demonstrate "commitment" to their new profession and the "will" to succeed in it. Becoming eligible was a lifelong project, while the consortium's support was limited in time and in its nature. The alternative to training was to self-resettle, to move with minimal assistance off land that the government, the World Bank, and the consortium described as belonging to the state.

Resettlement functioned as a type of dividing practice (Foucault 1982) that separated people who were primed to succeed in a more fully market-based economy from those who were not. The labels of *éligible* and *non-éligible* made this point rhetorically; they came to stand for different types of people, and they gave people a way to understand themselves and others. These categories were byproducts of the consortium's efforts to extricate itself from the rehabilitation of farmers, and not the result of its commitment to the formation of neoliberal subjects.

The consortium distributed responsibility for resettlement and its outcomes across a network of actors: NGOs were supposed to advise farmers about their resettlement options and retrain them; local authorities were expected to negotiate access to land with farmers; and farmers were charged with self-resettling, assessing markets, selecting training programs, starting new businesses, and investing in their own rehabilitation. The consortium and the World Bank's monitoring bodies chalked the failure of the programs up to personal attributes such as the lack of "will," "commitment," or "goals," or to poor decision making, alcoholism, or the inability to manage money. The consortium instituted "improved" consultation processes and intensified monitoring procedures that underscored the limits of its commitments and provided opportunities to disengage and cut off benefits, and farmers could never do enough, work hard enough, or invest wisely enough.

With the implementation of the *LUMAP* land mapping exercises in 2007, farmers' calculations shifted abruptly. Farmers' primary concern was no longer becoming eligible; instead it was about staking claims to as much land as possible, since these claims were recorded in the consortium's database and used to identify recipients of compensation payments. By walking the perimeters of their plots, farmers staked claims to land, established the boundaries of their fields, and claimed the rights to trees. This does not mean that the claims they made as part of the *LUMAP* exercises were any more objective or "true" than their earlier self-reports. The results of the *LUMAP* reflect the contingent outcomes of ongoing disputes over land and the ability of people to stake a claim to land at a particular moment in time (Berry 1993). The idea that some of these claims were provisional, that contests over land continued, and that the consortium's database was not a definitive record of landownership in the oil field region was underscored by a "data note" that appeared in the *LUMAP* reports themselves:

> In comparing data between tables and years, inconsistencies in numbers are due to the ever-evolving nature of the data (more fields belonging to M. Ngar . . . have been measured in another village; a "dependent" who, with further information, turns out to really belong to another HH). The overall messages delivered by the tables in this document remain the same, despite slight increases or decreases. The tables have been calculated as of December 31st, 2012 whereas the data keeps evolving. (EEPCI 2013, 2)

For the purposes of capturing compensation and resettlement benefits, the claims farmers made were preemptive in the sense that there were no guarantees that the land claimed as part of the land mapping exercises would ever be expropriated. The consortium's introduction of the *LUMAP* in response to a public relations crisis made it more difficult than it had been for farmers and their families to become eligible for resettlement benefits and to recover from the loss of land. The land mapping exercises produced a land registry and effectively privatized land, but without assigning private title to farmers. The *LUMAP* made land use and land tenure arrangements less flexible and dynamic than in the past, even as it allowed the consortium to downsize its resettlement programs and withdraw from resettlement activities while suggesting to the public that the impacts of the project were not as severe as farmers had reported.

FOUR

Ties That Bind

On a hot July day, not long after the land mapping exercises had begun as part of the *Land Use Mitigation Action Plan* (*LUMAP*), I was standing with Ngondoloum in the middle of the dirt road that bisected the village. Off to our left, a crowd had gathered around the edges of Daouda's concession. Daouda was at the center of the crowd, and several of his neighbors were standing in three corners of his concession, pulling on ropes until they were taut. Daouda looked down the lines formed by the ropes like a field surveyor, directing the person at either end to move slightly to the right or left. When they all agreed on the position of the ropes, another man walked the length of them with a long stick, carving lines in the dirt. I asked Ngondoloum what the men were doing. "Marking the boundaries between their concessions," he said.

"Why?" I asked. It was not as if the consortium was going to take land in the heart of the village. Ngondoloum explained that Daouda and his neighbors had seen the consortium's field agents measure and mark their fields and had decided it would also be a good idea to establish the boundaries of their land inside the village.

The pipeline project privatized land in the oil field region. The process of privatizing did not happen through the court system or a set of legal proceedings, and no one received title to land or became an official landowner.[1] It happened through the actions of farmers like Daouda and the men holding the ropes and drawing lines in the dirt. They were copying the consortium's field agents who measured, counted, and mapped their agricultural land. Initially the agents had measured and mapped only the land the consortium needed for the project at the moment of expropriation. But as part of the *LUMAP*, which began in 2007, the consortium collected information about the entire land base of villages, whether the land was slated for expropriation or not. The mapping exercises facilitated the consortium's task of acquiring land for the project in exchange for one-time cash payments but, more important, it allowed the consortium to respond to public concerns about the effects of land takes on families and to produce its own data on the land resources available to residents rather than allowing farmers' self-reports to shape media coverage of the project. In responding to these demands of the consortium to make their claims legible, people had to restructure their ties to land and to one another.

Despite the scene at Daouda's concession, residents did not take up the idea of private property or the calculative logic embedded in the *Compensation and Resettlement Plan* in exactly the ways the consortium had imagined they would. They did not jettison kinship and social relations in land or the obligations and forms of sociality those ties entailed to become private landowners and autonomous economic agents who used the compensation payments to replace lost items through the market. Neoliberal projects are not totalizing (Ellison 2009; Molyneux 2008; Shever 2008), and people in the oil field region adopted the calculative rationality and the market logic the consortium introduced via the plan, but in partial and unexpected ways. On the same day we watched the scene in Daouda's village, we drove to another village in the canton. On that drive, as on many others, Ngondoloum told me whose land was passing by in the window. "Ca c'est pour les Oundadé," he would say, or "Cette parcelle appartient à la famille de Philipe." In Ngondoloum's narrations, land belonged to families: *"les* Oundadé," in the plural, or *"la famille* de Philipe." Even after the project began, people continued to talk about land through the idiom of the family, and to lay different histories of the land alongside one another. The process of privatizing land that occurred through the *Compensation and Resettlement Plan* transformed relational subjectivities and reconfigured person-land relations, but it did not rupture the affective ties or social relations Ngondoloum referenced as we sped along the road.

In this chapter, I show how kinship, familial relations, and social networks were remade by the values the consortium assigned to everyday objects, the land mapping exercises, and people's responses to them. I show how families divided their landholdings and allocated plots to individual family members in preparation for the consortium's agents, and how this process created new categories of people and forms of identity. In intrafamilial negotiations over land, people designated themselves and other family members as "primary rights holders" and "dependents." They re-created themselves as either people who could extract value from the land—especially the value the consortium attached to land-clearing labor, crops, and trees—or people who could not and therefore depended on others for assistance and support. I also show how families used family meetings and advice-giving sessions known as *conseils de famille* to allocate payments in ways that recognized and reinforced family ties and were more palatable to extended family members than the winner-take-all provisions of the *Compensation and Resettlement Plan*. These methods of distributing payments recognized affective attachments, but they also transformed these attachments by reading them through the terms of the plan.

Affective relations facilitated the work of the consortium and the process of social and economic transformation in a region already in the throes of economic transition (Magrin 2001). It was possible to think of the oil field region as a "nearly neoliberal site" (Molé 2010) in the sense that people could anticipate a future when they would no longer be able to live off the land and would have to be more fully integrated into market economies. Families in canton Miandoum were not subsistence farmers when the project began, despite claims to the contrary in the media and elsewhere. They had long been immersed in cash economies and were dependent on markets for food and other basic necessities. Self-sufficiency in staple grains was still a goal, though an increasingly elusive one, and its achievement was worn like a badge of honor and seen as evidence of hard work and moral virtue. Consortium staff did not make this off-farm future explicit or talk about the effects of the pipeline project in this way, and the project did not bring this vision to fruition, but the anticipation of it shaped affective relations and the psychic experience of the project.

In anticipation of this future, conversations in canton Miandoum frequently circled around the topic of displacement and how the consortium wanted people to leave their villages—but on their own and without its assistance. People said the consortium was slowly pushing them out by taking more and more of their land and surrounding their villages with wells, roads, high-voltage power lines, gathering stations, and other installations. The fact that the consortium's agents never discussed the futures of the villages at the heart of the project only fueled suspicion that these villages were scheduled for elimination, but elimination by attrition or slow death, as they were gradually transformed into unlivable spaces. The question was only how long families could hold out. I once asked Gregoire, who had trained to become a mason and was complaining about a lack of work, why so few people in Ngalaba were building houses with durable materials like cement blocks, baked bricks, or tin roofs. He repeated what I had heard from many others: no one believed they would be able to stay in the village, so why invest in a nice house?

What was important about these statements was not their veracity, but their capacity to reveal how apprehension and anxiety circulated and attached to people who were—or might be—investing their money outside the village. This took many forms, but in this chapter, I focus on the anxiety that attached to married women who farmed their own fields. People worried that these women, who were eligible to capture compensation payments, might use the payments to break free of the village and marital ties. Patrilocal residence was practiced throughout the region, and questions about women's allegiances to their marital families transcended the pipeline project. Women were routinely reminded who they were "working for" and how the fruits of their labor should be allocated when they farmed land belonging to their husbands' families, and they were suspected of siphoning food and other resources from their fields and marital homes for the benefit of their natal families in other villages. The possibility of windfall payments amplified these concerns. The consortium, following the lead of its staff anthropologist, imagined men and women to be equally capable of working the land and therefore equally capable of capturing the payments. Yet, the effect of the compensation program was to severely compromise women's access to land and to transform women who farmed their own fields into figures of suspicion and doubt at a time when women's independent production had become increasingly vital to household bottom lines.

The expropriation of land strained social ties, but it also strengthened them. It led to new forms of inequality within and between families and it exacerbated existing ones, particularly along the axis of gender. Affective ties worked to facilitate the project and social and economic transformation in multiple ways, but without molding subjects into the kinds of individuated and autonomous market-based agents the consortium imagined. The consortium depended on families to allocate their landholdings to individual family members, to absorb the work of distributing compensation payments, and to manage the tensions and conflicts this work produced. By bearing these burdens, families smoothed the implementation of the project and even allowed the consortium to complete construction on the pipeline and begin producing oil a full year ahead of schedule.[2] People had to reconfigure their ties to land to fit the demands of the compensation program and the land mapping exercises. But the program and the exercises papered over the familial ties and affective sentiments that made them possible and that complicated the claims in the consortium's databases, embedding those claims in ongoing social relations.

Marking Boundaries

The consortium's scheme to expropriate land was designed to adhere to Chadian laws and the World Bank's standard on involuntary resettlement (EEPCI 1999b, vol. 3, sec. 1.6; World Bank 2004). The Chadian land laws the consortium adopted date from the colonial period and claim land in the oil field region for the state. The consortium used these laws to suggest that farmers were "customary users" of state land who were entitled to payment for "improvements and investments" in the land, but not for the land itself (EEPCI 1999b, vol. 3, sec. 5.1; Guyer 2002). Under the World Bank's standard, the consortium was responsible for providing displaced farmers with the replacement cost of lost assets, minus the land itself. Compensation took the form of one-time cash payments that were supposed to cover the cost of clearing a "replacement" field and buying food on the market until the next agricultural cycle. The payments were also supposed to cover lost income, amortized over a number of years, from trees that were cleared, as well as the cost of replacing sheds, beehives, and other structures.

The consortium was also responsible for providing information to people about the value of their assets and how they would be compensated. It conducted market surveys and used those surveys to establish compensation rates for field labor, food crops, cotton, trees, beehives, dwellings, and latrines. The rates were known collectively as the *barème,* and they were published in the *Compensation and Resettlement Plan* and printed on the land transfer contracts farmers received when their land was taken. Consortium staff and nongovernmental organization (NGO) activists encouraged farmers to learn these rates and to take an active role in calculating the value of their plots, as in this excerpt from the plan:

> Any farmer who is to receive compensation for a field will measure the amount of land for which compensation is due. Because fields are laid out in cordes, a farmer can survey his or her land by finding the midpoints of the sides of the field, determine perpendiculars from the midpoints, and thereby divide the field into one-quarter cordes. The farmer can then repeat this process to determine one-eighth cordes.
>
> Use of this method avoids subsequent accusations of mis-measurement or miscalculation of square meterage. Fields were clearly marked out with survey stakes and were measured by using GPS survey equipment and by complying with the land requirements for the OFDA [Oil Field Development Area] and the thirty-meter easement requirements along the pipeline. The data were recorded and converted into AutoCAD, and drawings of each field were generated. (EEPCI 1999b, vol. 3, sec. 5.3.1)

Encouraging farmers to count, measure, and calculate was supposed to streamline the compensation process and ensure that land transfers proceeded smoothly by confirming the measurements the consortium obtained through the use of precision technologies like global positioning systems survey equipment and AutoCAD maps. The consortium's aim in having farmers calculate their payments was to circumvent "accusations of mis-measurement or miscalculation of square meterage" and avoid "contention" over the size of the compensation payments. It was supposed to rationalize expropriation and make it more efficient and less contentious—at least for the consortium.

While most people did not measure their land in exactly the way the consortium advised, the compensation program changed the way people in the oil field region thought about land and everyday objects. Measuring, calculating, and counting transform their objects; they turn the intangible into the tangible (Miller 2001), and they "translate the invisible and qualitative into visible and quantitative 'facts'" (Kornberger and Carter 2010, 331). People counted trees and came to see fruit trees as "productive" or "nonproductive," shade trees as "young" or "adult," and different species of trees as more or less valuable. People contested the consortium's designation of fallowed land as "bush" and argued that there was no longer any unclaimed land in the canton, but they also came to read the landscape as composed of "fields," for which the consortium would pay individual compensation, and "bush," for which it would not. The *barème* changed the way people saw individual plots of land; it made some plots more attractive than others. Residents kept plots that would yield large compensation payments under cultivation, and they fought over high-value plots of land, the borders of their fields, and the rights to claim valuable trees.

With the implementation of the *LUMAP*, people had to preemptively stake individual and exclusive claims to land, as though it were private property. Families had to divide up their landholdings, define the boundaries of adjoining plots, and apportion land to individual family members who had to present themselves as the owners of these demarcated plots whether or not the land was slated for expropriation. They had to show their land to the consortium's agents, who followed them as they walked the perimeters of their plots and who mapped and measured their land and registered it in a proprietary database where no overlapping claims could be recorded. The consortium drew up contracts for land with individual farmers who received cash payments as sovereign beneficiaries and who had to decide for themselves how to allocate the payments. This process atomized and isolated farmers; it alienated them from their families and obscured social relations in land. But not entirely.

I happened to be visiting Temadji on a day when the consortium's agents were going door-to-door in her village, taking people to their fields to measure, map, and register their land. I found her lying on a mat on the ground in front of her house, sick and visibly shaken. Temadji told me that she had recently gone to one of her fields to find that her cousin Paul, who lived next door, had put up tree branches to mark the boundaries of their adjoining fields. In marking his field he had encroached on hers and staked out a segment of land that was roughly twenty by one hundred meters. There were three *karité* trees on this small segment of land, including one "productive" and two "nonproductive" trees. Temadji used the consortium's designations to describe for me the trees on the contested patch. She was upset that Paul had put up boundary markers and had not approached her about the land or the limits of their fields, but had instead presented his case directly to the chief of the village, who was also a cousin.

Paul told the story differently. He said he went to the chief because Temadji grew up outside the village and did not know the proper limits of their fields, which he had farmed since he was a young boy. Their fathers had cleared the fields and farmed side by side as young men, but Temadji's father had left the village and spent most of his adult life as a pastor assigned to preach in faraway places. He occasionally came back with his family, but they never stayed long. When Temadji returned to the village with her parents in 2000, her father was too old to farm. Before he died in 2002, he showed Temadji his land. Paul said the family had given Temadji and her mother full use of her father's plots, but neither woman had the force to clear much land. They did not have a plow or a team of oxen, Temadji's mother was old and tired, and Temadji was sick and had little interest in farming—points Temadji did not dispute.

Paul also said that before Temadji's father died, he had asked him to take care of his daughter. Temadji was divorced and in her forties, with grown children and brothers who lived elsewhere. After Temadji came back to the village, she started getting thin and weak. She spent several years looking for treatments, and going as far as N'Djamena to consult doctors. On the day I visited her, Temadji was lying on the mat because she had been suffering from another bout of dysentery that had already lasted four days. She complained that no one had come to see her or bring her food, and that relatives who lived all around her had abandoned her. Pointing in the direction of Paul's house, she said that in their last conversation Paul had reminded her that he would hold her funeral ceremonies in his concession.

Temadji had to break off her account multiple times to catch her breath. Each time, she shook her head, as if in disbelief, and repeated that she found the whole incident "shocking." She was anxious and uncertain about what she should do when the consortium's agents arrived at her door to take her to her fields. Should she show them the patch of land with the trees and insist that it was her land? Or should she cede her claim to it and let Paul claim the land he had marked off with the tree branches, since she clearly depended on him and needed his assistance?

The project, and especially the taking of land for compensation, transformed the physical and the psychic landscape of the oil field region. It turned the intangible into the tangible. Family land with fuzzy boundaries became a twenty by one hundred meter plot with one "productive" and two "nonproductive" karité trees whose value could be calculated. Familial relations and sentiments influenced the way people responded to the changes the project introduced and at the same time facilitated those changes. Analiese Richard and Daromir Rudnyckyj (2009) argue that affect, which in their lexicon refers to relations practiced between people, or a form of "action upon action," creates new kinds of subjects and new relations between them. It is both reflexive and intersubjective, acting simultaneously on those who perform it and on those upon whom it acts so that subjects are mutually formed or constituted through their relations. This process of subjectification or subject creation facilitates social and economic transformations and is not just a response to them (see also Shever 2008).

What allowed Paul to successfully claim the land with the valuable trees was not brute force or his superior knowledge of the boundaries of the plots (Carrier

1998). In fact, Paul and Temadji produced witnesses whose competing claims about the limits of their plots were never reconciled. It was instead his ability to enact, through his relationship with Temadji, the kind of subject the project imagined and sought to produce that worked in Paul's favor. He was able to show himself—to produce himself—as a detached and calculating person who could establish himself as an independent rights holder by measuring and marking the limits of his plot, who could invest his labor in the land and make it productive, and who could thereby transform land into a "field" and capture its value in the form of a compensation payment. Paul's ability to make the land legible to the consortium as a field and to extract value from it through his labor constituted him as a particular kind of person, one who was capable of taking care of himself and others—including Temadji. These actions and the boundary dispute simultaneously produced Temadji as a qualitatively different kind of person, the kind the consortium referred to as a "dependent"—one who was neither productive nor capable of taking care of herself and needed Paul's help, care, and support.

Affect structures possible courses of action or the ways relations between people might unfold. But it does not determine these actions, and it is never possible to fully predict the form action will take. Richard and Rudnyckyj (2009) draw attention to the contingency of neoliberal projects and to the uncertainty of the outcomes of these projects. In marking the boundary of his family's plots and claiming the contested plot of land for himself, Paul did not separate himself from Temadji; he neither adopted the logic of private property nor emulated the imaginary figure of economic man. Instead he publicly bound himself to Temadji, underscoring his kinship with her and the obligations that relation entailed. Paul reminded the chief and other members of their extended family of his responsibilities for Temadji and his obligations to her father: to provide Temadji with land, to take care of her, and to hold her funeral ceremonies in his concession. He also acted on those claims. In the years that followed the land mapping exercises, Paul continued to take Temadji to her medical appointments on the back of his motorcycle and to send his children to her concession to help her with chores and bring her food.

But the incident with the boundary markers and the land mapping exercises also transformed their relationship, and it was this transformation that Temadji found shocking. It literally took her breath away. When the consortium's field agents came to Temadji's house, she walked the perimeter of her plot as Paul had marked it. But even after she ceded the twenty by one hundred meter plot, Temadji continued to pick the nuts from the "productive" tree that was registered to Paul in the consortium's database (and was never expropriated). I read her actions not so much as a way to stake her claim to the tree as a way to stake her claim to Paul and to his continued support, underscoring her dependence on him. The work done in families to allocate land in ways that distinguished those who could make the land productive from those who could not and that established new types of relations between these categories or kinds of people helped the consortium carry out the land mapping exercises. It facilitated the consortium's efforts to privatize land and to construct a comprehensive database of individual land claims, to take land and distribute compensation payments efficiently, and to present itself to a skeptical public as operating in a way that minimized the project's impact on local populations.

Settling

The consortium signaled its intention to expropriate land by marking it off with survey stakes. Shortly after the land was marked, farmers received a land transfer contract and a one-time cash payment. The consortium's land transfer agents dispensed advice about how to use the compensation payments to those who received them as if the farmers identified as the recipients of the payments were autonomous actors, freed from the webs of sociality that tied people to each other through land.

The consortium's agents impressed upon farmers the need to take responsibility for themselves and their families, to manage land and cash wisely, and to rely on the market, and not the state, the consortium, or NGOs, to recover and get back on track. People who received compensation payments were advised to manage the payments to cover their needs over extended periods of time. The payments were supposed to last a full growing season in the case of purchasing food supplies, and to cover the loss of income from fruit trees, the payments had to be managed over a number of years. The consortium's local community contacts, staff anthropologist, and land transfer agents repeatedly reminded farmers about the intended uses of the payments and warned them about the hazards of "wasting" money on alcohol and bride-price payments. Farmers were encouraged to consider the option of taking in-kind compensation in the form of plows, bicycles, building materials, and sewing machines if they thought that saving, planning, and budgeting would be difficult.[3]

The consortium's quarterly and annual progress reports, which were intended for English-speaking audiences outside Chad, provided regular updates on the compensation program. They included information about changes in the compensation rates and the sums of cash paid out in the previous quarter and over the life of the project, and also profiled some of the recipients of the payments and depicted them as the kinds of ideal rational economic actors the project sought to produce. Take, for example, the two farmers profiled in the consortium's 2011 annual report. One is a young man identified as Ngaradoum Frederic from the village of Begada 1. The report contains a photograph of Ngaradoum with a caption that reads, "I use my land to grow sorghum, peanuts, and beans. The project took 1/16 of a hectare and I have 1/4 hectare left. I am happy to receive compensation because I will buy an ox to help me grow more crops and earn more money." Beneath the photograph of Ngaradoum is one of Denebeye Agathe, a woman from the same village. The caption below her photograph reads, "The project needed 1/16 of a hectare of my land, which is right next to Ngaradoum's plot. I have received several compensations from the project before, and I have about 1/2 hectare of land now. With the previous compensations, I used the money to build a house and buy 2 oxen which had a baby, so now I have even an additional ox. This money will pay for food for my 16 children, who all live with me now" (EEPCI 2011, 38).

Ngaradoum Frederic and Denebeye Agathe appear in the report as successful beneficiaries of the consortium's compensation program. Each knows the precise amount of land the consortium took, down to one-sixteenth of a hectare, and how much land remains in their personal holdings. Each made an autonomous decision about how to invest the cash received from the consortium, and each made a productive investment, spending money on basic necessities like farm animals, a house, and food. Some of these investments have already paid dividends: Denebeye's oxen "had a baby" so now she has "even an additional ox." Ngaradoum's investments promise future wealth in the form of "more crops" and "more money." But the accounts are as interesting for what is absent as they are for what is present. There are no family members in these accounts, except for the sixteen children (a predictably fantastic number) that Denebeye describes as dependents—the people for whom she will buy food. Ngaradoum Frederic and Denebeye Agathe appear as superhuman agents of their own lives who calculate their landholdings; grow sorghum, peanuts and beans; buy oxen; build houses; feed large numbers of children; and manage compensation payments all on their own.

The consortium's efforts to dismantle kinship and make it invisible were not limited to the farmer profiles it published in its progress reports; they were also discernible in the *Compensation and Resettlement Plan* and in the compensation process itself. The only lines in the 153-page plan that address the question of how the consortium would identify the beneficiaries of the compensation payments read as follows, "Compensation will be paid to the individual who holds primary rights in the field, *i.e.,* who had the field cleared. This individual will be responsible for settling with anyone else who is farming in that field" (EEPCI 1999b, vol. 3, sec. 5.3.3).

The consortium structured the compensation program so that a single person, the person "who had the field cleared" in the season it was expropriated, had "primary rights" in the field and therefore to the payment. This person was responsible for taking into account anyone else who might have been farming in the field. Such a formulation of rights in land expedited the expropriation of land; the consortium did not have to pause its operations to make sense of complex kinship ties or dense webs of relations expressed through land. But familial ties and affective relations resurfaced and were renegotiated and transformed through the process the consortium euphemized as "settling."

Settling usually occurred in family gatherings or meetings known as *conseils de famille*. Families in the oil field region hold *conseils de famille* to discuss marriage proposals, funeral arrangements, plans for schooling and initiation, and many other collective matters. But once the pipeline project began, *conseils de famille* were also held to decide how the cash from the payments should be used, to offer advice and counsel to family members who were about to invest the cash payments, and to manage or repair social relations strained by disputes over land and cash. People took up the work of settling in families and in the *conseils de famille* because the alternatives were unpalatable. Consortium staff and local authorities could not help families decide how to allocate the payments and could only repeat the dictum that the person who cleared the field had the right to the payment. People described this solution as *sec*—as too dry, harsh and definitive.

Family members traveled, sometimes from as far away as N'Djamena or Maiduguri, to attend family meetings where the allotment of large payments was discussed. Meetings were not convened for small payments (generally payments of less than 100,000 or 200,000 francs) because it was agreed that these sums were so small that the recipients could use or distribute them as they pleased. When someone received a large payment, it was important for him or her to present the payment to the family when it was still *integral* (whole)—before any of the cash had been spent. I often heard people explain the failures of small business ventures by saying that the compensation money was invested without first assembling family members and listening to their advice.

A critical part of the *conseils de famille* was retracing the history of the land and remembering and naming the people who had used it in the past. In sharing and recounting these histories, families elaborated and reinforced their ties to others. But familial relations were also transformed as families read their ties to each other through the provisions of the *Compensation and Resettlement Plan*. Family members traveled to find elderly relatives and to consult them about the history of the land and the trees and to verify kinship claims and claims to the payment. The *barème* figured prominently in these family discussions. The *conseils de famille* often started with talk about who had planted, cared for, and harvested the trees that appeared on the land transfer contracts. People who had planted or tended to the trees were ascribed rights to the payments, since trees were the most valuable items in the *barème* and the money for them made up the bulk of most payments.

The receipt of a payment was an occasion for relatives to visit the village, or to write to the recipient of the payment and renew contact with the family, to remember their shared ties, and to remind the recipient to think of them when allocating the payment. But the person who received the compensation payment from the consortium retained a privileged position in the negotiations even if he or she had only farmed the land in the year it was expropriated, because families adopted the notion that without the individual's efforts the land would have been "bush" and there would have been no payment at all.

Families drew elements of the consortium's logic into their lives and into the *conseils de famille,* but they never adopted this logic completely. They used the monetary values the consortium attached to things, such as "the price of the trees," as reference points in their discussions, but families did not allocate the payments according to a strict formula in the way the consortium did. In fact, there was considerable variation from the *barème* in terms of how the payments were allocated. The settling process invites comparisons to Barbara Yngvesson's (1976) work on styles of responses to interpersonal grievances in small-scale communities, and her claim that grievances tend to be settled privately and informally when enduring relations are important. In these situations, when the aim is "healing," or maintaining harmonious relations, there is tolerance for a wide range of outcomes around an ideal norm. The rules and rationalities the consortium introduced were guideposts, not straitjackets. Many of the settlements I witnessed or heard about appeared patently unfair or unequal, but they were considered successful by family members because all pronounced themselves satisfied with the outcomes.

Still, the allocation of the payments was not easy, and the task was approached by many people in the families I followed with trepidation and a sense of dread. Farmers rarely held on to the payments for extended periods of time—not because they spent impulsively, but because they worked to organize family meetings and rid themselves of the cash quickly, almost always within weeks of receiving the payments. In the interim, they described themselves as tormented, unable to sleep, and filled with gnawing anxiety. People described the cash as evil or diabolical, as a source of discord and unhappiness. While families tried to avoid disputes and aimed to settle them in ways that would satisfy everyone, this was not always possible, especially because families were expropriated multiple times over the course of the project, and the repeated payments and family discussions were complicated by the layering of affective claims.

One of the family feuds I followed pitted Isaac, who was among the oldest men in the village, against his daughter, Odette. The consortium's agents gave Isaac a payment for a field Odette had farmed because she was away from the village at the time of the expropriation. When Odette received news of the payment, she interrupted her trip and returned to the village to ask her father for the cash. Isaac proposed to call a *conseil de famille* and to distribute the payment among family members. But Odette preempted this plan by complaining to the chief of their village that the payment should be hers since she had farmed the field and that Isaac had only received the cash because she had traveled.

As word circulated about the family dispute, people in the village were critical of Odette's use of the consortium's rules and of the village chief, who could only comply with those rules, to extract the payment from her father. But Odette described her decision to seek the chief's help in recuperating the payment as a way to teach her father a lesson. Before the consortium took the plot Odette farmed it had taken another family plot from Isaac. He had given the money from that plot to Lonondji, one of his youngest daughters, without calling a *conseil de famille* or consulting anyone. On hearing the news, the family convened a meeting to confront Isaac and to counsel him about his behavior. Isaac's eldest son, Eli, complained that Lonodji was only a young girl. What would such a young girl do with 200,000 francs? Odette reminded her father that she and her siblings who were present at the meeting would be the ones who would take care of Lonodji after he died. Had he forgotten that? The other children told their father that what he had done was "not normal," and they chastised him for not thinking of them. His method of dividing the compensation money showed, they said, that he loved Lonodji best. Isaac's brother urged him to give the rest of the money to the children who were present at the meeting, but Isaac said he had no money left.

The consortium's policies established certain forms of person-land relations and rights claims as legitimate, in part because local authorities had to recognize and endorse them. People found the consortium's formulations harsh and inappropriate, but there were also times when the dry and definitive rules of the consortium were invoked. The consortium's policies provided tools with which people like Odette could manage affective relations and discipline family members for failing to recognize relational ties. The consortium's policies allowed Odette to remind her father of his responsibilities and obligations to all of his children, and of their mutual obligations to each other, when it would not otherwise have been permissible for a child to challenge a parent in that way. They allowed her to reprimand her father for failing to distribute his previous payment in a way that family members thought was fair and that preserved familial sentiments, and to show Isaac what he should have done by distributing the recuperated payment to multiple family members, including himself. The policies therefore made new forms of agency and affective relations possible.

The compensation program both disrupted and disturbed affective relations and solidified and strengthened those relations. The process of "settling" and the *conseils de famille* reanimated kinship and affective ties, but it also transformed those ties, though not in exactly the ways the consortium imagined. Recipients of the payments and their families prioritized family reconciliation and the maintenance of familial bonds over individuation and economic rehabilitation, and they worked hard to maintain those bonds, even though it meant "settling" in ways that diverged, sometimes dramatically, from the *Compensation and Resettlement Plan* and the consortium's line-item valuations and models of economic recovery. The allocation of payments was the source of family feuds, but it also led people to remember and retrace the history of the land though through the prism of the plan. People reinforced their ties to each other through the exchange of notes, stories, visits, and cash, and their ties were transformed by the "price of the trees" and the *barème*, as well as ideas about "fields," "bush," "primary rights," "dependents," and "settling."

She Puffs Herself Up

The physical presence of the project and the consortium's ongoing expropriation of land contributed to worries about the long-term viability of the villages of the oil field region. This anxiety about the future coalesced around the compensation payments, who received them, and how they were used. I frequently heard stories about farmers using compensation payments to buy land and build houses in Bébédjia, a town twenty kilometers to the north of Miandoum. People claimed that money was being secreted out of the village and that people were quietly buying land, building houses, and preparing their departure. Evidence of these kinds of transfers was hard to come by, however. When I asked people how they spent their compensation payments, they typically provided long, finely detailed lists of modest expenditures: five thousand francs to a sister, ten thousand to a wife, soap, sacks of grain, tea, sugar, and school fees. Those who received larger payments might report buying a bicycle, a motorcycle, farm implements, or an ox. With the exception of a few people who worked for the consortium, I never encountered anyone who bought land or built a house outside the village, and most of the compensation payments provided only a fraction of the cash that would be needed for this purpose. A handful of families moved during the period of the project, but the populations of the villages remained remarkably stable despite rampant speculation about their imminent demise.

Sara Ahmed (2004) suggests that affect does not reside in a person or a thing but is produced in the circulation between objects and signs. The stories about people funneling money out of the village were not attached to specific people, but they created a profile of the kinds of people that came to be objects of fear, suspicion, and doubt. These stories regrouped those who could take wealth—not oil wealth, but wealth in the form of compensation payments—out of the village, aligning them with others who could do the same and pitting them against everyone else. In principle, anyone who farmed and was therefore eligible to cap-ture a payment was a potential defector. But some people or groups of people were more suspect than others. This included farmers who received particularly large payments, men whose connections to the village were traced through ma-ternal and not paternal relatives, and married women, whose attachments to their natal families were suspected of trumping their attachments to their marital fam-ilies and villages.

Jean and John Comaroff (2001) describe occult economies as accompanying the expansion of "millennial capitalism," a form of late capitalism that produces wealth through speculative financialization and through which people get rich without performing any kind of productive labor. The windfall compensation payments, which "fell" on the residents of the oil field region in a seemingly ran-dom and unpredictable manner and without any advance warning, produced sud-den wealth that fueled fear and anxiety about the accumulation and circulation of capital and suspicion and doubt about the intentions of the recipients. Accusations of sorcery were not new in the villages of canton Miandoum, and it was impos-sible to gauge whether they rose or fell in frequency with the introduction of the pipeline project. But what was remarkable during the period of the project was how accusations were consistently leveled at people who collected large payments—usually payments of millions of francs. This circle of farmers was small and consisted almost exclusively of young and relatively affluent men who reinforced suspicions about their intentions to move when they bought motorcy-cles that allowed them to travel. The wealthiest farmer in one of the villages where I worked, who also happened to be linked to the village through his maternal relatives, was accused of sorcery and chased from the village when it was revealed that he planned to use his payment to buy a car—the ultimate symbol of freedom, independence, and mobility.

Ahmed suggests that signs increase in affective value the more they circulate, so people and things can appear to possess or contain affect even though these objects "come to life not as the cause of anxiety but as an effect of its travels" (2004, 125). In the oil field region, anxieties about the future coalesced most strikingly around married women who farmed their own fields rather than the small pack of superrich men. These women were not suspected of being witches, but they were thought of as potentially fickle domestic partners whose real allegiances lay elsewhere.

Rodrique and Minga were both in their sixties and headed up a large, extended family. They lived in a sprawling concession at the edge of the village that backed up on one of the consortium's gathering stations. During one of my visits to their concession, the three of us were talking about women who farm their own fields. What follows is part of our conversation, reproduced from my field notes:

R: Certain women are with their husbands, but want money, and they
   are the ones who do their own fields. Women with their husbands who do their own fields, it is to send money to their villages. The day there is a conflict between the woman and her
   husband she will go to her natal village.

M: If I had strength, I would cultivate with my husband, but now
   what I can do is cook for my husband.

R: My daughter in Kyraté, it was only this year that she wanted her
   own field because she suffered a lot. She was forced to sell the
   seeds of peanuts [that she had saved to plant] because the rains
   were late, so now she is growing sesame. I appreciate what my
   daughter is doing because she works with her husband, but
   after the harvest her husband always sells the harvest, and so
   she decided she would have her own field and use the money
   to feed her children.

L: Does she have problems with her husband?

R: Since they have been married they have not fought, but the only
   problem is that her husband sells the crops after the harvest.

L: What does he do with the money from the crops?

R: We live in different villages, so I don't know what he spends the
   money on. I don't have a problem to give her some of my land.
   For widows there is no problem to work in their own fields. For
   other women I don't think it is a good idea.

It is difficult to sort through the tangle of ideas about women who farm their
own fields that emerges from this short segment of conversation. Rodrique seems
to contradict himself at every turn. He says women farm their own fields because
they want money, but that his daughter farms to take care of her children. He
claims to appreciate what his daughter is doing, but he also asserts that farming
alone might be acceptable for widows but is not a good idea for a married woman
like his daughter. Personal fields and the women who farmed them were places
for the layering of ideas and associations that ran in all directions.

Rodrique's narration draws on a history of shifting ecological conditions and
land tenure relations in the oil field region that was not explicitly referenced in our
discussion but was entangled in intrafamilial struggles over land. Well before the
project began, people in the region divided their agricultural fields into two categories: household fields (the generic, default category) and personal fields. Personal
fields, or *champs personnelles,* were fields farmed by a single person and operated
under market principles. The history of personal fields is embedded in the colonial-
era policy of mandatory cotton cultivation, a different type of extractive project

in which colonial authorities required every adult in canton Miandoum, and throughout most of southern Chad, to farm one *corde* of cotton in each agricultural season (Magnant 1986). Cotton quickly degraded the soil, and farmers were regularly ordered to clear more of the forest to create new plots (Cabot 1965). The adoption of draft animals and plow culture, popularized by missionaries in the 1950s as a way to help farmers keep up with the labor demands of growing both food and cotton, further accelerated the pace of deforestation. As early as the 1950s, geographers attached to the colonial government expressed alarm at the speed and scale of deforestation taking place in the south and encouraged the colonial administration, and later the Chadian government, to begin planning for what even then was a foreseeable need to intensify agricultural production in response to looming land shortages (Bardinet 1977; Cabot 1955, 1965; Gilg 1970).

Decades before the pipeline project began, the introduction of mandatory cotton cultivation on a per-head basis brought about the idea of some fields as personal or individual. In the half century between 1930 and the disappearance of the forest in 1980, personal fields became an important source of wealth for women in canton Miandoum who initially cleared the plots to grow cotton and later used them to grow cotton or food crops for cash. Women who were particularly prosperous farmers were known as *baou déné*. In Ngambaye, *baou* is a word for someone who is rich or who has many things, and *déné* means woman.[4] The *baou déné* cleared land and passed it on to their children, but they also used cash from the sale of cotton or food crops to buy draft animals (whose offspring are still in use), they married their sons and nephews by paying the bride-price for their wives, they contributed food to their natal and marital households and, in some cases, they supported their husbands and children and were the primary providers for their families. Many men in canton Miandoum live in their mothers' or grandmothers' villages or work the land they inherited from these women, even though the Ngambaye are classified or described as patrilineal.

The idea that women in southern Chad once farmed autonomously and controlled the crops they produced figured prominently in the consortium's descriptions of local livelihood strategies and social organization. The consortium said that fieldwork conducted by its staff anthropologist showed that 60 percent of women farmed their own fields (EEPCI 1999b, vol. 3, app. B), and the consortium suggested that since so many women participated in farming and agricultural markets, the *Compensation and Resettlement Plan* would be gender-neutral in the sense that men and women would receive compensation in proportion to the labor they invested in the land. The minority of women who did not farm personal fields would be covered by household resettlement policies that treated them as dependents of other household members who did farm. But what the authors of the plan failed to take into account was that the period between 1930 and 1980 now seems like a remarkable interlude in the history of the rural south. Women's relative autonomy and their ability to cultivate on a par with men was not a durable cultural fact—as the consortium assumed in the plan—but a historical anomaly made possible by a particular set of conditions and especially the availability of unclaimed land. Over the preceding half century, land pressure and changes in the local ecology of the oil field region had reduced flexibility in land tenure arrangements in ways that concentrated control over land in men's hands. The compensation program exacerbated this trend.

The authors of the plan also failed to recognize that attaching value to crops, trees, and other objects through the application of the *barème* would set off a scramble for land that would further transform the ability of some groups, and especially married women, to access land. The compensation program changed access to land and land use in ways that were deeply gendered. Table 4.1 shows the distribution of land in each village by gender and type of field for the 2010–11 agricultural season. During that season, I tracked how members of the eighty families I followed used their land, because I had repeatedly heard that women were rushing to cultivate personal fields and positioning themselves to capture compensation payments yet, at the same time, women complained that their husbands refused to give them access to land and even refused to allow them to intercrop on family fields because they were worried about them becoming *baou* (rich).

The table shows whether the plots were put into cultivation or held in fallow, whether they were cultivated by the household as a household field or by an individual as a personal field, and how personal fields were distributed by gender.[5] For the 2010–11 agricultural cycle, the eighty families I followed retained a total of 962 plots. Crops were planted on 564 of these, or on 59 percent of landholdings. The intensity of land use recorded in the table exceeds even the most optimistic estimates of the ratios of land in cultivation to land in fallow needed to maintain soil fertility.[6] Land use was most intensive in the sites where the consortium took the most land, or where project facilities were concentrated and the consortium was most active. The patterns of land use reflected the shortage of land in sites at the epicenter of project operations, but they also reflected the relative likelihood of expropriation, and how land use was shaped by the anticipation of expropriation and the efforts people made to make land legible to the consortium as "fields."

Table 4.1 also shows the gendered effects of the compensation program on land use and suggests that gender relations can vary over space as well as time (Massey 1994), even within a region as small as canton Miandoum. Especially in villages where land expropriation was not only possible but likely, it was men, and not women, who succeeded in positioning themselves to capture land and the

Table 4.1. Land use by village, 2010–11 agricultural cycle

Village	Ngalaba (n = 40 hhs)	Maikeri (n = 20 hhs)	Bendoh (n = 20 hhs)	Total (n = 80 hhs)
Consortium designation	High impact	Moderate impact	Low impact	
Total number of plots	509	257	196	962
Plots farmed	334 (65.6%)	158 (61.5%)	73 (37.2%)	565 (58.7%)
By women (personal)	43 (12.9%)	21 (13.3%)	13 (17.8%)	77 (13.6%)
By men (personal)	149 (44.6%)	66 (41.8%)	20 (27.4%)	235 (41.6%)
By households	142 (42.5%)	71 (44.9%)	40 (54.8%)	253 (44.8%)

payments. Of the 565 plots cultivated in the 2010–11 agricultural season, only 77, or 13 percent, were farmed by women as personal fields.[7] The proportion of women in the villages who farmed personal fields is not shown, but it was far below the consortium's preproject estimate of 60 percent (EEPCI 1999b, vol. 3, app. B). In comparison, 235 plots, or nearly 42 percent of all plots, were farmed by men as personal fields, and an almost equal number of plots were farmed as household fields. In the villages most heavily impacted by the project, men were more than three times as likely as women to be farming personal fields, and it was only in the "low-impact" village of Bendoh that the number of household fields—the default category before the project began—far outstripped the number of fields farmed by men as personal fields.

What the data in table 4.1 suggest is that men staked claims to land and to the compensation payments by farming land as personal fields to the detriment of household fields, fields cultivated by women, and fields that lay fallow. This pattern of land use shaped and was shaped by gendered subjectivities. People in the oil field region still subscribe to the normative ideal of personal fields as sources of discretionary income for men and for women but, as the conversation about Rodrique and Minga's daughter suggests, food and cash generated from personal fields are almost always diverted to meet basic household needs. Women's access to land and to cash was required for households to function, but it was also a source of anxiety. These anxieties about women's allegiances—who they were "working for"—escalated dramatically with the introduction of the windfall compensation payments.

No one could predict in advance what plots of land the consortium would expropriate next, so farming a personal field always carried with it the possibility of capturing a windfall compensation payment and becoming *baou* overnight. People talked about women who farmed their own fields as inflated with self-importance, using verbs like *se bombé* (she puffs herself up) or *se glorifie* (she glorifies herself, or she lords it over us). Throughout the period of the project, women who farmed their own fields were described as decadent, dangerous, and disrespectful, or as people who liked modern things like city clothes and nightlife and who only cared about amassing money. Pastors in the village churches railed against married women who farmed alone, and people denounced women who supposedly rushed to stake out personal fields and position themselves to capture compensation payments. These women were accused of precisely the kinds of things Rodrique first mentioned—trying to store up money and make investments in their natal villages so they could make a life for themselves free of their husbands and in-laws.

The same set of contradictory associations that was attached to women who farmed personal fields in the present was also attached to the women who had farmed them in the past. I stumbled onto this in conducting life histories with older women who were once *baou déné*. Many of these women were hesitant to talk about their past as wealthy and successful farmers. One eighty-year-old woman began her story in a confessional mode, leaning into me and saying, almost in a whisper, "As a Christian, I need to tell you the truth. I was a *baou déné*." Other women broke off their stories as others joined us or passed within earshot. When I asked people for help in identifying women who had been *baou déné*, some people refused to cite the names of women in their villages as though it would be slanderous to do so. But alongside these encounters were others in which the *baou déné* and their grown children spoke proudly of granaries bursting with millet, the draft animals these women had purchased whose offspring were still used to plow fields, the land inherited from long dead but still revered grandmothers, and the wives these women had married for the family.

The difficulties women had in accessing land also affected their ability to capture compensation payments. Between 2000 and the end of 2007, my colleagues and I tracked who received compensation payments and how they were used, and our records include information on nearly eleven hundred payments. This represents most of the payments made during this period to the residents of three villages. Table 4.2 shows how the payments, which totaled roughly 330 million francs, or approximately US$660,000, were distributed by village and gender.

Not surprisingly, the allocation of payments by gender mirrors the allocation of land. Men captured most of the payments, and they captured most of the total cash paid out in compensation. This was even (and especially) the case in the village with the fewest cases of expropriation. Men and women differed not only in their ability to occupy the land and capture the compensation payments but also in their ability to use those payments to accumulate wealth or to shore up familial and social ties. Women who captured payments were able to retain less money than men who captured payments. Funds received by women were distributed to

Table 4.2. Compensation paid in three villages, 2000–2007

Village	Ngalaba	Maikeri	Bendoh	Total
Consortium designation	High impact	Moderate impact	Low impact	
Total number of payments	673	321	105	1,099
Payments to men	524 (78%)	252 (79%)	84 (80%)	860 (78%)
Total compensation paid[†]	215	103	12	330
Compensation paid to men[†]	165 (77%)	79 (77%)	12 (93%)	255 (77%)

[†] Millions of FCFA (rounded to nearest million).

a restricted set of recipients, and they mostly took the form of large payments to the men who granted them access to land. In contrast, men's cash payments were distributed in the form of small amounts to large numbers of kin.

As men secured land by farming it and by formalizing their claims to it with the consortium, it became more difficult for women to shore up their ties to natal (or marital) kin in the way the *baou déné* had once been able to do, notwithstanding widespread anxiety about women funneling wealth out of their marital villages.[8] The older women I talked to who were once *baou déné* made it clear to me that they were now just old women talking about the distant past. The *baou déné* no longer exist, except in memory. Their extinction went hand-in-hand with changes in the landscape of the canton and of the rural economy that foreclosed the possibility for women to accumulate wealth and shore up social relations by claiming and working the land.

To be successful in the time of oil, women had to be traders or *baou mosso*. But the term itself conveys the idea that wealth in the present is ephemeral—*mosso* means 'to fall down' or in this context to lose one's capital. Many women, and especially those who could not access land, practiced small trade to contribute to the household. *Mosso* was the term people used to describe the kind of small trade women practiced. It involved selling small quantities of peanuts in plastic wrap, oil stored in old water bottles, or balls of sugar, salt, or tea, and working on the thinnest of margins. The demise of these enterprises was inevitable; hence the term *mosso*. Small trade and falling down—as in going broke—went together. Used in conjunction with *mosso, baou* is a misnomer because women regularly 'fall down,' and while they might be able to 'get back up,' they are not able to accumulate wealth.

The *Compensation and Resettlement Plan* was not gender neutral. Women were marginalized by the oil economy and moved off the land. They were depicted as outsiders and potential defectors in their marital villages, and the plan deepened their isolation and their dependence on men.

Ties That Bind

In the oil field region, new kinds of subjects and affective attachments were created as families allocated land based on who could extract value from it and who could not. This sorting process functioned as a form of subjectification, creating people as "primary rights holders" and as "dependents," as those who could extract value through their labor versus those who needed the support of others. The mapping of the land in the region proceeded seamlessly because this work had already been done in families by the time the consortium's agents arrived at farmers' doors.

The consortium's land expropriation scheme privatized land in the oil field region, but the idea that people could claim land as private property and use individual compensation payments and markets to rehabilitate themselves in the ways the consortium envisioned was complicated by affective relations and enduring entanglements with others. James Ellison (2009) has noted that multiple forms of subjectivity arise out of neoliberal projects and that the types of subjects these projects produce are in no way self-evident or foreordained. The policies elaborated in the *Compensation and Resettlement Plan* did not produce the kinds of individuated, autonomous, calculating, and self-actualizing subjects the consortium profiled in its progress reports or bring about a complete break from past forms of social organization (see Shever 2008). In fact, it reinforced relational ties while at the same time refracting and transforming those ties through the prism of the plan.

Families rejected the consortium's model of rights to compensation as too clear-cut, definitive, and harsh, and their attempts to find more palatable formulas for distributing the payments took place out of sight of the consortium and its agents. The *conseils de famille* were sites for remembering and remaking social ties through discussions about the allocation of payments. "Settling" was a complicated affair. The plan structured conversations and the allocation of payments, but it was flexibly applied. Those who planted or cared for trees or transformed land from "bush" into "fields" assumed privileged, but never fixed, positions in the negotiations over the payments, and gender was a primary axis of difference. The *Compensation and Resettlement Plan* also made new forms of agency and new ways of relating in families possible, as Odette's use of the consortium's rules to govern family relations demonstrates.

Family ties also shaped access to land and payments. People could apprehend an off-farm future, even if this transformation was incomplete and never realized during the period of the pipeline project. Fear and anxiety about the future was attached to those who might escape or defect—especially married women who farmed their own fields; solo farming became difficult and dangerous for married women even as it became vital to household economies. The consortium's anthropologist and the authors of the plan neglected to consider how growing land pressure and changes in the local ecology affected access to land, which was happening even in the absence of the project but was exacerbated by it. They imagined men and women as equally capable of clearing fields—a case of viewing "culture" as static and of crafting policies based on outdated ideas about livelihoods and forms of social organization (see Gilberthorpe 2013). The plan altered gendered subjectivities and ideas about what it meant to be a proper woman and wife in the present and in the past, shaping the distribution of land and payments in ways that intensified women's dependent relations with men and complicated strategies for household provisioning and poverty reduction.

The consortium's decision to respond to a public relations crisis by mapping land and creating a comprehensive database of people and their landholdings transformed person-land relations, family ties, and relational subjectivities. People reconstituted kinship and social ties to fit the consortium's demands; they made individual claims to plots of land, and they took up some of the policies, terms, categories, and ideas the consortium introduced through the *Compensation and Resettlement Plan*. But the project did not preclude people from maintaining and even strengthening their ties to others or from recognizing others' claims to the land, the payments, and to relatedness and belonging. Even if they were scrubbed from the consortium's databases, familial entanglements in land were not erased.[9] By taking up the tasks of distributing land and cash in the *conseils de famille* and managing the fall-out from these exercises—which became increasingly complicated as expropriations multiplied—families facilitated the implementation of the pipeline project and allowed the consortium to operate efficiently. Affective ties and family sentiment helped propel social and economic transformation and moved the project forward.

FIVE

In the Midst of Things

The oil field region is just over six hundred kilometers from Chad's capital city of N'Djamena. When making the trip, especially in the early years of the project, I often got caught behind long, slow-moving convoys transporting heavy machinery, building materials, and supplies for the project. The convoys sometimes stretched for miles; they snaked along what was then a two-lane dirt road and kicked up so much dust that even in the middle of the day the driver had to turn on the headlights to see the road ahead. Most of the material for the project arrived via the port in Douala, Cameroon, and had to be transported overland to the consortium's base camps in the south of Chad. The consortium stockpiled the steady stream of incoming cargo in massive warehouses and outdoor supply yards scattered around the oil field region. Some of the things in those convoys were expected to have short lives (Kopytoff 1986), like food and the domestic supplies consumed by workers in the camps. But the consortium expected other things to live on—in some cases indefinitely. When the project ended in 2025 or sometime thereafter, the consortium planned to leave the wells and buried pipeline in place, turn the power plant over to the government, and give buildings to local organizations or dismantle them and recycle the parts (EEPCI 1999a).

A major preoccupation of the consortium was how to secure all of this equipment and material. The consortium was concerned about theft and the possibility of sabotage and it was also concerned about safety and restricting third-party access to hazardous chemicals and other materials. The pipeline project in Chad was like other extractive industry projects in that the consortium and the Chadian government assembled a massive security apparatus to maintain order in the oil field region. The consortium hired thousands of private security agents to guard installations and conduct patrols and surveillance along the roadways. These agents were backed up by military police, who also conducted patrols and surveillance as well as raids and house-to-house searches for missing materials. At work sites, the consortium set up checkpoints and implemented protocols to prevent workers from appropriating supplies. Local authorities controlled the movements of residents by imposing curfews. The project paired these conventional security measures with innovative design and technical and engineering solutions to minimize the likelihood of property damage or loss.

Yet while the consortium was preoccupied with securing equipment and materials for the project it was also concerned about getting rid of things once they were no longer useful. The project generated thousands of tons of waste each year, including everything from mattresses, used tires, and automobile parts to wood packing crates, segments of pipe, scrap metal, and lubricating oils. The treatment and disposal of so many things posed risks to the environment that the consortium was mandated to manage under its agreements with the World Bank. The consortium developed a comprehensive waste management plan that emphasized efforts to minimize waste and to recycle. The plan included a program to recycle nonhazardous waste into local communities where people might find uses for the items the consortium no longer needed. The consortium and World Bank monitors described this program as an instance of corporate philanthropy—as a "donation program" (ECMG 2005, 32)—and not as dumping, even though it transferred thousands of tons of material from its camps to the surrounding villages each year. The waste management plan also incorporated global standards for operating landfills and incinerators and protocols for treating and disposing of dozens of different streams of waste in ways that were "environmentally acceptable" (EEPCI 1999b, vol. 5, sec. 1.0). The External Compliance Monitoring Group (ECMG), traveled regularly to the oil field region to monitor the consortium's implementation of the plan.

The consortium treated property and waste as separate categories, each with distinct protocols, networks, logics, and rationales. But the two were never as sharply delineated as the consortium imagined. Material artifacts from the project were everywhere—in people's houses and concessions, in markets, on the backs of bicycles and motorcycles, on the sides of roads, and in agricultural fields. The status of the things the project set in motion was indeterminate and ambiguous: What was property, and what was waste? In most cases the answer to this question was impossible to pin down.

The indeterminate status of the items in circulation complicated the efforts of security forces to maintain order by keeping things in their proper places. The systems of power and authority governing both property and waste overlapped in the oil field region and came together differently at different moments and in different places (Korf, Engeler, and Hagmann 2010). Their relative weight also varied over time and space, so that no one set of norms and rules predictably governed the objects in circulation or applied on a particular roadway or in a particular village. The coexistence of competing systems of power and authority—one governing property and the other governing waste—made the oil field region an uneven and unpredictable place, full of surprises and unexpected events (Korf et al. 2010; Watts 2004b). The simultaneous imperatives to secure objects as property and to manage them as waste produced substantial risks for people, but also some opportunities.

There are different ways to look at the problems posed in the side-by-side implementation of security and waste management protocols; in this chapter, I take an object-centered perspective. The objects that circulated in the region were active agents that did things. People who received project waste tried to secure and stabilize the meanings of the things in their possession, but they were never successful. Objects reflect back on the people who possess them (Reno 2009), and most of the materials that circulated in the oil field region retained traces of their former identities as the property of the consortium. As liminal objects or objects still in transformation they reflected back on people in ways that were particularly dangerous (Douglas 2002). If there was uncertainty about the status of an object, there was also uncertainty about the status of the person who possessed it. The question of what was property versus what was waste foreshadowed another: Who was a thief, and who was a beneficiary of the consortium's community recycling program? Both questions were ever-present and were sources of a pervasive tension in the oil field region.

The ambiguous status of the objects that circulated erased the distinctions between project and nonproject spaces. The project was designed to avoid the need for displacement, so project infrastructure wound around villages and did not breach them. The objects that circulated blurred these lines and transformed canton Miandoum into a space of surveillance, making it possible for security forces to not only penetrate and search villages and houses but to conduct these operations on schedules that were erratic and completely unpredictable. People stayed off roads and away from installations and as far from project activities as possible, but they could not avoid the reach of things.

Project-related objects provoked intense and sometimes contradictory feelings and reactions. People liked the community recycling program, and they worked to acquire and maintain the consortium's cast-off things. But they also feared and loathed the objects that emanated from the project and worked to distance themselves from them. They refused to pick them up or allow them in their houses and they removed them from their villages, buried them underground, and threw them in the dirt in disgust. People kept objects away to avoid inviting scrutiny and suspicion and to distance themselves from the active agency of objects to define them as thieves or beneficiaries. Residents rejected both categories and insisted that what the consortium gave them was waste, or objects that had no value (Halperin 2003). As active agents in the oil field region, objects enabled what John Frow has called "moves in subtle games" (2003, 25). Donated objects helped residents read what the consortium thought of them and what they were worth (Reno 2009); they also allowed residents to send their own messages back, and to define themselves for themselves as well as for others—including the consortium.

Securing Property

One of the most striking features of the oil field region, and of extractive enclaves everywhere, was the omnipresence of security and surveillance (Ferguson 2005, 2006). The equipment and materials I followed on those slow-moving convoys were stored in supply yards surrounded by chain-link fence topped with rolls of razor wire. Thousands of private security guards watched over the supply yards and company property around the clock. Buses filled with guards rumbled through villages at the time of shift changes, and in town, swarms of off-duty personnel congregated on the streets outside the offices of Copgard and Garantie, the companies that employed them. Private security agents were posted at storage and processing facilities, wells, rigs, supply yards, and construction sites where materials and machines were left overnight. They were backed up by military police and soldiers that the government dispatched to the region. Private security agents alerted government police to suspicious activity via a shared channel on their two-way radios, and the consortium supplied the police with fuel to respond to these calls and to conduct patrols and surveillance activities (IAG 2002a).

Local authorities also tried to secure the region by restricting people's movements. Visitors were expected to present themselves to local authorities and to show government-issued travel authorization. These formalities were carried out throughout the country and were not specific to the oil field region, but in the region authorities probed visitors about the motives for their travel with extra zeal. (I was once asked to get approval from the governor for my visit.) NGO activists complained that they were denied access to the region at critical moments in the project, such as when a pipe burst and there was an oil spill on a farmer's field, but the restrictions on residents' movements were the most severe. The governor issued multiple curfews that confined people to their villages after 6:00 p.m., and the head of the government's security forces for the oil field region, who occupied the newly created post of *directeur de la sécurité et de la protection des installations pétrolières,* issued decrees prohibiting all motorcycle travel in the region because operators of motorcycle taxis were suspected of being conduits for the transport of stolen materials from villages to nearby towns.

The consortium tried to minimize theft and damage to property by building security into the project's design. The pipeline was built almost entirely underground, where it could not be easily damaged or destroyed. The consortium instituted a well pad antitheft program that involved reengineering fittings and equipment to make them more difficult to damage or dismantle, and even proactively damaging fittings—"marring" bolts—to make them difficult to remove as well as less useful or appealing (ECMG 2012a; EEPCI 2008a). Transformers were placed inside locked cages, and antennas were mounted on steel poles encircled with razor wire. The consortium also instituted a number of workplace routines to prevent employees from stealing company property: vehicles leaving the base camp were searched, and refueling teams were prohibited from making stops between the drilling rigs they serviced. At critical points in the project the consortium set up checkpoints along roads and searched all vehicles for stolen materials.

Yet despite the surveillance and the layers of security, the consortium was never able to stop the theft of project materials. There was a lively black market for diesel fuel and gasoline in regional towns; soap, bottled water, protective eyewear, work boots, cables, and building materials circulated informally and were traded and sold in local markets. Occasionally, expensive equipment would go missing—things like solar panels, transformers, or pumps that kept oil wells in operation. People who lived in canton Miandoum insisted that the perpetrators in these cases had to be consortium employees with technical training rather than the laborers hired from the villages, since only people who worked for the consortium and had access to specialized markets outside the oil field region would have the skills and know-how to dismantle and offload these items. People were arrested and sent to prison for stealing from the consortium, but the consortium's efforts were mostly focused on deterring theft rather than prosecuting it.

Managing Waste

When equipment and materials were no longer useful to the consortium, they were supposed to be processed through the Komé Waste Management Facility. The facility was the central node in the consortium's waste management system. From the facility waste was distributed to landfills, incinerators, leachate collection systems, burn pits, and local communities. Project waste was supposed to be collected at the facility and sorted and treated according to procedures described in the *Waste Management Plan,* a document that was part of the project's overall *Environmental Management Plan (EMP).* The consortium described the plan as a "cradle-to-grave" system to manage waste, from the site where the waste was produced to the location of its "ultimate disposal" (EEPCI 1999b, vol. 5, sec. 4.0.2).

The plan was part of an effort to respond to public pressure on the oil and gas industry to develop cleaner modes of operating, especially in places like Chad. It was modeled after "industry best practices and internationally accepted standards and guidelines," and it provided a road map for managing waste in ways the consortium described as "environmentally acceptable" (EEPCI 1999b, vol. 5, sec. 1.0). The document began with this set of guiding principles for minimizing project waste:

Where practicable, all personnel should seek opportunities to minimize the amount of waste generated through the use of process
changes, raw material changes, or other commonly accepted waste
minimization options. The waste minimization concept can be sum-
marized as the following hierarchy:

- If possible, don't generate the waste.
- If generated, try to recycle/reclaim the waste.
- If it can't be recycled/reclaimed, treat it to "destroy" the waste or
  render it non-waste like.
- If there is still a waste, dispose of it in an environmentally accept-
  able manner. (EEPCI 1999b, vol. 5, sec. 1.0)

The plan included instructions for handling specific types of waste as well as
descriptions of the consortium's waste-tracking system, the technologies that
would be used to treat and dispose of waste, the types of waste storage units available at the Komé Waste Management Facility and how they would be selected,
and the operating plans for the facility's incinerators and landfills. A key feature of
the plan was a "community recycling program," which was designed to minimize
the consortium's environmental impact by recycling nonhazardous waste into local communities, where some of the consortium's cast-off objects might be put
to creative reuse. The recycling program put thousands of tons of material and
hundreds of thousands of project-related items into circulation every year. In fact,
in most years for which data are available, more project waste was donated to local
communities than disposed of in any other way.

The consortium's waste disposal practices and its compliance with the waste
management procedures set out in the plan were monitored by the External Compliance Monitoring Group, which was hired by the International Finance Corporation to make regular monitoring trips to the oil field region. The difficulties of
minimizing and disposing of waste were recurring themes in the ECMG's reports.
The group described chronic delays in the construction of landfills and incinerators. Over the life of the project, the ECMG described waste piling up in the camps
and the consortium scrambling to find ways to get rid of it. The monitors commented on the accumulation of hundreds of thousands of liters of used lubricating oil, mounds of "putrescible food waste" (ECMG 2007, 26), and stockpiles
of hydrocarbon-contaminated soils and recyclable wood and packing crates
waiting to be processed through the Komé facility. The ECMG described drums
and other waste containment systems as "overpacked" (2005, 32). Even after
construction of the landfills and incinerators at the Komé facility was com-

pleted there was insufficient capacity to handle the volume of waste produced by the camp, which the ECMG described as "equivalent to a small municipality" (ECMG 2003a, 46).

The ECMG's reports are full of references to the difficulties of breaking down waste and of eradicating it or making it disappear. Waste disposal methods are never perfect (Edensor 2005), and it is apparent in reading the plan that the consortium expected to have to deal with waste even after it was processed and treated. The opening lines of the plan refer to matter that cannot be destroyed or rendered "non-waste like." The plan provides instructions to workers for handling specific waste streams that emphasize the special efforts required to keep buried tires from floating back to the surface and leachable metals and other hazardous wastes from escaping their containment systems and polluting the environment.

An alternative to eradicating waste is to remove it from view (Gille 2007), but the consortium also struggled in this regard. At one point, ECMG monitors reported that the consortium pumped 250,000 liters of used lubricating oil underground using an injection well "as a contingency measure to resolve an emergency situation" (ECMG 2003b, 41), while noting that 500,000 liters of used oil remained in the camp while the consortium searched for places to put it. The consortium disposed of food waste that was accumulating faster than it could be processed by donating it to a local pig farm and through open-air burning, despite the impact on air quality in and around the base camp (ECMG 2003b).

Construction of the landfills and incinerators that were part of the Komé Waste Management Facility was completed in 2004, after the pipeline was already built and the period of peak employment and activity had ended. From 2005 on, the consortium provided estimates to the ECMG of the volume of waste processed through the facility each year. In 2008, for example, the facility processed ten million kilograms of waste—roughly twenty-two million pounds, or eleven thousand tons—which was slightly more than the previous year (ECMG 2009). While the numbers give the illusion of precision, waste is difficult to measure (Gille 2007), and it was never clear what sources of waste were included and what sources were missing from these figures, since substantial amounts of waste were buried at work sites or generated and processed by subcontractors without transiting through the Komé facility. The consortium's accounting was also difficult to follow, as this excerpt from a 2012 ECMG report shows: "According to the information provided, the total amount of waste produced at the OFDA [Oil Field Development Area] during this period [October 2011 to October 2012] is equal to 6,022 tons, 3,173 tons were processed, 4,421 tons recycled, and 1,784 tons donated with 3,356 tons of excess waste in storage" (ECMG 2012b; 28).

Workers at the facility were tasked with sorting project waste into as many as forty different waste streams. The plan included protocols for processing batteries, concrete, asbestos, paint, medical waste, tires, glass, scrap metal, plastic and rubber, motor oil, paint, domestic trash, construction debris, and contaminated soil. For each waste stream, the plan included safety considerations for waste handlers, ideas about how to minimize that type of waste, and a decision tree to enable workers to determine how and where to dispose of the item and what kinds of tests might be needed to determine if the material was hazardous. The protocol for disposing of used tires suggested that the consortium would minimize the volume of cast-off tires by checking air pressure and wheel alignment on its vehicles, which reduces wear and extends the life of tires (EEPCI 1999b, vol. 5, sec. 2.1). It also indicated that spent tires might be used as packing material or protective cushioning in materials storage yards, that local populations could make shoes from tires, and that tires could be used for "pavement amendment" or to upgrade local roads. If discarded tires could not be used in these ways, workers at the facility were instructed to (1) send the tires to a tire recycler; (2) reuse them for erosion control or grind them for use in road materials or for some other purpose; (3) put them in a nonhazardous waste landfill; or (4) bury them on site while taking measures to make sure they would not float to the surface.

If the consortium could not eradicate waste, it could track it and know where it was located. According to the plan, every movement of project waste was supposed to be documented. When waste left the Komé facility it was accompanied by a "waste manifest form" signed by the people who generated, transported, and received that waste. The waste was sent to landfills, incinerators, burn pits, aboveground contained storage facilities, pit storage sites, or local communities (EEPCI 1999b, vol. 5, sec. 4.0.2). The waste manifest forms included information about the location of the waste, whether it was hazardous or nonhazardous, how much of it there was, and the type of container it was stored in. For waste buried at work sites there was a "waste burial record" that indicated the distance and direction of the bury pit from a landmark, such as a well pad. It documented the dimensions of the bury pit, and the material used to line it, and it provided a description of its contents. Waste sent out for testing was accompanied by a "chain-of-custody form" that documented how the waste sample was handled and who held it on what dates. Copies of these forms were forwarded to a database manager who was responsible for "waste tracking" (EEPCI 1999b, vol. 5, sec. 2.0).

Every year, millions of kilograms of nonhazardous waste were donated to local villages as part of the consortium's community recycling program (ECMG 2005). This is how the consortium described the program in the *Waste Management Plan*:

Another option that exists for reuse of a material after it has been generated is to recycle it into the community if it has a beneficial reuse. This option exists because materials which may be considered to be 'wastes' by Project personnel may still have intrinsic value to individuals in the local communities.

When it is safe and practical to do so, materials of value to the community will be made available to the community for reuse. Note that only non-hazardous materials will be recycled into the community. (EEPCI 1999b, vol. 5, sec. 5.0)

The consortium donated "domestic" items such as plastic, metal, and aluminum containers, glass, and packaging materials as well as "construction debris," "scrap iron and other metal materials," and objects discarded after tuneups on project vehicles, like tires and inner tubes (EEPCI 1999b, vol. 5, sec. 5.0). The consortium suggested that people might convert "wood waste, pallets, and packaging" into "firewood" or "art object[s]" or use them for "general construction and carpentry." According to the consortium, leftover segments of pipe might be used for "general construction" but also for "rainfall drainage" and "fencing."

The consortium regularly dumped donated waste in front of the chief's house in Miandoum. Materials like scrap wood and iron were also left in borrow pits (ECMG 2004) or at construction sites on land adjacent to agricultural fields where farmers were actively working. The consortium also organized special donations of items. After a freak windstorm battered canton Miandoum, the consortium delivered piles of scrap wood for families whose houses had sustained damage. It also gave wood, used nails, and scrap iron to farmers who became eligible for resettlement and who enrolled in training programs to learn off-farm trades in carpentry and welding. Displaced farmers who participated in the training programs in improved agricultural production methods received fencing materials to protect seedlings and build chicken coops. The consortium donated wood to schools and churches to make tables and benches, and to collectives whose members wrote letters requesting materials for various projects.

Given the volume of material the consortium donated to local communities, it was not surprising that project waste was everywhere in canton Miandoum. In a spot survey we conducted in 2008, sixty-three of the eighty households I followed had at least one form of project waste in view in the family concession, and in many concessions multiple forms of waste were lying around. People converted scrap wood from shipping pallets and packing crates into doors, windows, tables, and chairs; they hung plastic strips of yellow or red construction tape side by side in doors and windows as curtains; they made cooking pots from melted scraps of

Scrap wood donated following a windstorm.

Tape reading CAUTION CONSTRUCTION AREA used as a curtain.

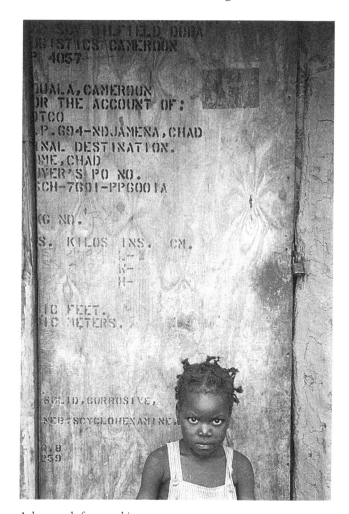

A door made from packing crates.

aluminum, and reused nails after straightening them on discarded engine blocks. They fenced kitchen gardens, ringed young trees, and decorated graves with remnants of wire mesh; they used segments of pipe as chairs or benches in family concessions and in the cabarets where people met to drink millet beer. Plastic tarps covered holes in their roofs or were used as floor mats, and shipping containers were converted into classrooms, shops, and offices. These and many other materials—scrap metals, sacks, raincoats, pails, ladders, barrels, safety goggles, gloves, flagpoles, hard hats, hammers—were on display in family concessions.

A discarded shipping container converted into an office for the chief of the canton.

The consortium counted on public and private security forces to secure property and prevent theft at the same time they were releasing a continuous stream of waste into the communities of the oil field region. Surveillance to prevent the theft of property and the program to mitigate the environmental impact of the project by recycling nonhazardous waste into communities unfolded side by side. The simultaneous imperatives to secure materials (as property) and to dispose of them (as waste) gave way to two very different logics or rationales for treating objects and the people who possessed them. The coexistence and entanglement of these competing systems of power and authority—one governing property and the other governing waste—blurred distinctions between project and nonproject spaces, opened up nonproject spaces to monitoring and surveillance, and produced substantial risks for people as well as some opportunities.

The Shifting Nature of Things

On one of my trips to the oil field region, I arrived in Ngalaba the day after a police raid. I found Bessandji, who was the head of one of the families I followed, sitting in front of his house with his head in his hands, looking dejected. The door to his house had been ripped from its hinges and was hanging by a single nail. The

Fencing material used to protect a young tree from animals.

police had come to the village at daybreak, before most people had gone to their fields. Bessandji and others described how the police had carried out a door-to-door search for property belonging to the consortium. If people were not home or doors were locked, the police broke them down. The police moved through the village, picking up items presumed to be the consortium's property and ordering people to carry these objects to the main road. People piled scrap metal, wood, wire mesh, barrels, jerricans, tarp, and other miscellaneous items into pickup trucks. The police struck two young men who protested that the materials

Tables made from work-site signs and recovered nails.

A school bus used to transport workers that was recycled into a local community but could not be repaired.

were items that the consortium no longer wanted, and they arrested a total of six people.

The raid underscored the lability of objects in the oil field region. The hazard for people who possessed objects generated by the project was the potential for the form and value of the object to change even if the object itself stayed the same (Alexander 2005; Appadurai 1986). The consortium converted property into waste in the Komé Waste Management Facility, but the raid showed that it was also possible for waste to become property (Reno 2009; Thompson 1979). The raid underscored how this potential crystallized at certain times and in certain places that were highly unpredictable. The raid was particularly shocking because villages, and especially family concessions, were spaces that people thought of as outside the ambit of the roving security patrols. But the theft of a high-value item the previous night—a solar panel had been removed from a well pad near the village—shifted the usual geography of surveillance and the relative ordering of the rationales of property and waste in ways that made it dangerous for people to have *any* material associated with the project anywhere near the scene of the theft.

In the days after the raid, people continued to protest that the things they hauled to the road and handed over to the police were things the consortium no longer wanted. They were waste, material that had no value (Halperin 2003). If the objects in family concessions were viewed as property in the eyes of the police at critical moments, as in the raid, it was not because people had managed to recommodify them (Thompson 1979). What the raid highlighted was the threat the fundamental ambiguity of things posed to the maintenance of social order (Hawkins and Muecke 2003). Keeping things in their proper places is vital to maintaining social order (Edensor 2005), and the private security agents and military police assigned to the region were preoccupied with the distribution of things in that space, especially when the consortium reported the loss of expensive equipment.

It was not always easy for security agents and the police to distinguish between what the consortium designated as property and what it designated as waste, and the ambiguous status of things also provided opportunities for security agents to extract cash or resources from farmers. Two pieces of wood that looked identical might have different statuses because of how the consortium processed them. One piece of wood could be classified as property at the same time the other was waste. Even when the status of an object was clear at a given point in time, as when people recuperated waste dumped in front of the chief's house, it did not stay that way. The objects the project set in motion had complicated histories (Kopytoff 1986). Objects moved from the Komé Waste Management Facility to the chief's house in Miandoum to family concessions to neighbors' houses to markets and back to other family concessions. They switched hands, families, villages, and uses. Some objects were recommodified and sold in markets, while others were not. The provenance of objects was lost in these movements and transformations, making it impossible for people to know what kind of object they had in their possession. This was in exact opposition to the precision the consortium strove for in its efforts to track, register, and situate waste. The technical precision and orderliness of the waste management protocols, the process of sorting waste into dozens of waste streams, and the manifests and registers the consortium used to record the weights and dispositions of things obscured the quirky trajectories of the objects that escaped these efforts to corral them and that entered into circulation alongside others in the oil field region.

The fact that project waste was everywhere in the region also contributed to the ambiguity of things. One of the ways waste is supposed to be differentiated from nonwaste is through its physical location. Waste is usually displaced or moved out of sight (Gille 2007). It is typically confined to a marginal space—such as a trash can or a landfill or the Komé Waste Management Facility—and to a space that is different from the space where the thing was used. In addition to sites marked for waste disposal, such as dumps and landfills, there are culturally specific ways of spatially segregating waste that convey its status to others. Zsuzsa Gille (2007) describes how in the United States, for example, placing an item on the curb marks the object as waste or trash and as available for the taking. In the oil field region, waste was at times delivered to the chief of the canton or to village chiefs, but it was also distributed in other ways. Here is an excerpt from the ECMG's report following its tenth monitoring visit to the oil field region:

> During the previous mission, ECMG observed that some borrow-pits in the OFDA area were used for making available scrap metal, concrete and wood from equipment packing to the local population. The ECMG encouraged this plan, but recommended improving the conditions and, to the extent possible, avoid possible hazardous conditions (presence of sharp metal scraps, nails, etc.) while handling these materials. During the 10th visit, the ECMG visited the reclaimed borrow pit area, where the innocuous waste had been buried and properly covered. The ECMG was also informed that the remaining material had been distributed safely to the population. (ECMG 2004, 25)

The consortium left waste in borrow pits for residents to pick up, and it was encouraged to do so by the ECMG. But borrow pits were not locations recognized in the plan or by residents as spaces for waste disposal. In fact, they were newly created spaces—sites scattered around the oil field region where the consortium excavated the earth to harvest sand, soil, or rock for construction projects. How were people to know that the scrap metal, concrete, and wood left in the borrow pits were waste and that they were free to take these materials? How were the private security forces and the police to know that these items were to be considered waste and were therefore available to all? Was everything left in a borrow pit considered waste? What about items left at other work sites? What was property, and what was waste?

Object Relations

The things that circulated in the oil field region were active agents entangled in the lives of people, and they helped to define the relations among them. Residents were acutely aware that the things they had in their possession reflected back on them (Reno 2009). If there was uncertainty or ambiguity about the status of an object, there was also uncertainty about the person who possessed it.

Residents tried to manage their identities in the midst of thousands of tons of material of indeterminate status, but this was never fully possible. Farmers took footpaths and back roads to their fields or to other villages and avoided the main roads whenever they could, especially if they were carrying objects that might be construed as the consortium's property, but slipups were common. Toward the end of one day, when we were driving from Maikeri toward Miandoum along a narrow dirt road, we passed a young boy riding a bicycle in the same direction. The boy was alone, and was riding at a leisurely pace. He seemed to barely take note of us. Then, all of a sudden, my colleague Ngondoloum gasped, flung his head out the window, and motioned frantically for the boy to get off the road. The driver stopped, while Ngondoloum screamed at the boy to ride inside the tree line where he would not be seen by passing security patrols. As the boy maneuvered his bicycle off the road and into the bush, I saw a piece of wood attached to the back of the bicycle with black rubber cords. No one asked the boy how he got the wood or where it came from, and the boy offered no explanation. In fact, he never said a word. What is property and what is waste? Who is a thief and who is a beneficiary of the consortium's community recycling program?

Project waste was particularly dangerous because of its liminal status as material in transition from one regime of value to another (Douglas 2002; Gille 2007). The cast-off items in people's houses and concessions, or strapped to the backs of their bicycles, clung to their former identities as the consortium's property. Even when people put objects to creative reuse, it was difficult to conceal or obscure their origins. Tables retained traces of their former lives as road signs or placards inscribed with the names and logos of subcontractors like Schlumberger. Doors and windows constructed from scrap wood were recognizable as recycled packing crates because they were stamped with English-language shipping labels and handling instructions. Some objects, like segments of pipe, were difficult to transform at all, and had to be reused in their original form. Objects that retained the identity of their former state—that were readily recognizable as the consortium's property—could always be perceived as matter out of place and a threat to social order.

On multiple occasions the consortium enlisted the help of police and local authorities to locate expensive equipment that had gone missing. In the raids and house-to-house searches that followed, like the one in Bessandji's village, the police confiscated items that were not, however, the things the consortium had reported missing, and used these occasions to arrest and fine farmers who had project waste in their possession. Before the start of a house-to-house search for a transformer in one village, local authorities and consortium staff called a meeting and encouraged residents to inform on people who stole from the consortium and to organize their own patrols to protect the nearby installations so future raids and searches would not be necessary. In fact, the consortium tried repeatedly to enlist residents in securing the installations around their villages.[1] These suggestions and the announcements of the house-to-house searches elicited scorn and anger. People asked rhetorically if the consortium was going to put them on its payroll, and joked about being taken for thieves by security agents if they approached the installations, especially at night. Their comments illustrate their awareness of the instability of the person-thing interface and of the potential for project installations to transform neighborhood patrolmen and volunteer guards into thieves and saboteurs.

Objects provoked a range of responses from people, including responses that were contradictory. Residents liked project waste and found it useful. They complained when waste was distributed to other villages but not to theirs, and they rushed to retrieve waste when it was made available. But at the same time, people feared and loathed the consortium's cast-off objects and worked to distance themselves from them. A man in one of the families I followed moved waste he acquired, which included typical items like segments of pipe, scrap wood and metal, and pieces of wire mesh, to his brother's house in Miandoum, which was farther from project installations and therefore less likely to be the site of a raid or search. When his brother came home and discovered the items, he panicked, dug a hole behind the house, and buried them. The brother who buried the items demanded that the brother who displaced them come to unearth the objects and remove them from his concession immediately. He also made it clear that no project waste was allowed in his house or concession.

Residents distanced themselves from project waste out of fear, and they resented the unpredictable intrusion of the police and security forces into their homes and lives. But it would be a mistake to view their responses to waste purely in terms of efforts to avoid being arrested or accused of stealing. They disliked the idea that they might be taken for thieves and that security agents took advantage of these opportunities to extort money from them, but they also resented the idea that the consortium's cast-off objects defined them as "beneficiaries."

Waste Dumps

Deliveries of waste from the Komé Waste Management Facility were not scheduled, so people never knew when the consortium's trucks would dump waste in front of the chief's house. But as soon as the trucks approached the entry to Miandoum, throngs of people would drop what they were doing and run after them to be present when the contents were disgorged onto the dirt field in front of the chief's compound. Pandemonium ensued. People grabbed objects and ran with them in all directions; some were pursued by the chief's security agents, who tried in vain to keep the crowds back. Away from these scenes, people accused the chief's security agents, the chief himself, and other local authorities of cherry-picking items before allowing residents to comb through the piles of rubbish. The prospect of finding useful materials in the waste lots was uncertain, and entering these melees was dangerous. Fights broke out over choice items, and people were pushed, shoved, knocked down, hit, and chased. People engaged in the contests over waste because they needed some of the things the consortium discarded, but they were also drawn by the opportunities the objects might afford (Reno 2009). No one knew what would be delivered in the next lot of waste or what they might miss out on if they were not on the scene when it arrived.

But even while people ran behind the consortium's trucks and scurried to grab prize pieces of wood or rare but useful items like mattresses, metal chairs and beds, ladders, and rain barrels, they never lost sight of the fact that they were chasing waste. The things that rolled off the dumping beds of the trucks were things that had no value to the consortium; they were things that were leftover, used up, or obsolete. The people who came to scavenge referred to the wood from packing crates as *déchet de bois* or *emballage perdu*—scrap or "garbage" wood. They complained that the chairs and tables they made from this cast-off wood did not last and were not as strong or sturdy as furniture made from local wood. Some of the things the consortium dumped, including large metal parts from earthmovers and machines used to drill wells, remained in place for months and even years because they were too heavy to move and people did not have the skills or equipment to transform them. Segments of pipe were always among the last things to be claimed, because people could not figure out what to do with them or how to break them down to form new objects. Some of the things people retrieved ended up lying in the dirt or weeds in their own concessions because the possibilities they anticipated for them never materialized. Waste sometimes remained waste. The waste dumps just transferred material from one location to another.

Not everyone rushed to claim items from the waste lots. Some refused to enter the fray or to pick up materials the consortium left behind, finding the prospect of chasing after garbage trucks and fighting over scraps of wood and metal and other throwaway objects demeaning and unseemly. An onlooker at one of these events told me he was standing on the sidelines because he was an *homme responsable*. He would not scurry after trash or allow himself to be chased by the chief's security agents; that would be shameful and humiliating. This was not to say that the materials held no interest for him, or that he did not see the potential utility of some of the things that were splayed across the field. But if there was excitement surrounding the waste dumps, there was also ambivalence about forming attachments to the consortium's waste and concerns about how it defined people vis-à-vis the consortium.

Frow describes the uses of things within social exchanges as "moves in subtle games, messages about the social categories to which I belong, the categories to which I claim belonging, and the categories I refuse" (2003, 25). The waste dumps gave people a sense of how the consortium thought of them and of what the consortium thought they were worth (Reno 2009) because of the kinds of things that were made available and the kinds of things that were withheld. Workers from the Komé Waste Management Facility shared stories with others in their villages about the computers, cars, and mobile homes the consortium dumped in landfills and buried underground.[2] Chadian workers were fired for trying to retrieve items from the landfills. One worker was dismissed for trying to extract used cables that he planned to strip for metals that could be made into jewelry. Another was fired for taking a cooler for storing ice. People wondered why the consortium would bury these things or throw them away instead of allowing workers or residents to have them, and why the consortium would only give them access to specific items—mostly items of limited value.

People read their relationship with the consortium through the objects the consortium donated to their communities, but these objects also allowed people to send their own messages. Objects were active agents that allowed people to distance themselves from them and from their capacities to mark people as thieves or beneficiaries. The man who described himself as an *homme responsable* was not prepared to humiliate himself by scrapping for garbage and being chased as if he were a thief. When I expressed interest in the cast-off objects in family concessions, people made a point of showing me how insignificant and meaningless they were. They picked them up and threw them down in the dirt, or they tossed them away from the house while asking what they could do with such a useless thing. Sometimes they pretended not to even see the object of my interest as a means of showing me just how inconsequential it was. Project waste rested in the weeds at the edges of family concessions along with household waste, and family members told me defiantly that it was all the same. When I asked to photograph objects, people laughed at the notion that the object could be important, have value, or merit that kind of attention.

Residents both scrambled to acquire project waste and worked to distance themselves from objects and their power to mark and define them. These were not grand, strategic actions (Certeau 2002); they were "moves in subtle games" (Frow 2003, 25).

In the Midst of Things

Objects in the oil field region were constantly changing status, as objects and matter do everywhere (Colloredo-Mansfield 2003). These value transformations were not the result of creative reuse or the emergence of new structures of value. They were tied, instead, to the fundamental ambiguity of things in a context in which thousands of private security agents and military police had a mandate to maintain order and prevent the theft of the consortium's property and sought ways to make a living from the project, where the consortium struggled to manage and dispose of thousands of tons of waste every year in accordance with environmental regulations, where monitors audited the consortium's adherence to environmental risk mitigation measures and helped the consortium improvise methods for dealing with waste, and where people had desires and aspirations for themselves that objects emanating from the project helped them realize.

The consortium's efforts to carry out the project in ways that were "environmentally acceptable" and to minimize waste by recycling nonhazardous material into local communities flooded the oil field region with things. Objects were discarded (or stored?) at work sites and deliberately (or mistakenly?) left behind in fields and along roadways. The way project waste was scattered across the geographic space of the oil field region blurred the usual spatial distinctions between waste and nonwaste, and it blurred the boundaries between project space and nonproject space such as villages and houses. Police and security agents ascribed certain types of person-thing relations to people with project-related objects, especially at moments when high-value items were missing, and especially in the geographic vicinity of the alleged theft. But even in the absence of these incidents, waste always had the potential to become the consortium's property, especially since it could not be completely transformed, and the people who had it in their possession could therefore always be taken for thieves. Objects marked people. This is how property and waste *worked,* even if the World Bank, the consortium, and the consultants charged with monitoring environmental risk mitigation thought of property and waste as distinct entities that had little or nothing in common.

In the accounts of project monitors, the status of an object depended on the well-defined set of procedures codified in the *Waste Management Plan*. For them there was no confusion about how any given object should be classified, tracked, or treated. There were protocols and infrastructure in place to manage property, and separate protocols and infrastructure to manage waste. The two categories were not considered within the same frame. The ECMG never broached the subject of property, even as part of a history of the waste streams it monitored. But conceived space—the abstract representation of the planner, the architect, or the social engineer—is not lived space, and efforts to plan and produce space are never fully realized. As Henri Lefebvre wrote, "even neocapitalism or 'organized' capitalism, even technocratic planners and programmers, cannot produce a space with a perfectly clear understanding of cause and effect, motive and implication" (1992, 37). Even if the planners and monitors acted in accordance with their own abstract representations of space because they believed them to be true, others—like the police who conducted the raids and house-to-house searches, the thousands of security personnel blanketing the region, the subcontractors who left waste in borrow pits, roadways, and farmers' fields, the objects themselves, which clung to their former identities, and the people who lived in the midst of these things— did not.

Property and waste were impossibly entangled in the oil field region. People had to navigate the uneven and unpredictable geography of property/waste. They had to learn to be ever vigilant, always on the lookout for the opportunities and the dangers presented by the shifting status of things.

SIX

Footprints

As an experiment in development, the pipeline project came to an end in early September 2008.[1] The World Bank's withdrawal from the project went mostly unnoticed in the oil field region; it made little difference to the activities of the consortium or in people's day-to-day lives. After 2008 the consortium continued to take and return land, pay compensation, and produce progress reports and post them to its website. People in the region continued to write letters to the consortium, visit the local community contacts (LCCs), and search for things of value in the waste dumps. The seamless continuation of the project after 2008 underscores Andrew Barry's claim that the "ethicalization" of business is not driven primarily by international institutions like the World Bank but is a project of business itself (2004, 196).

Following the World Bank's withdrawal from the project, the Independent Evaluation Group (IEG), an arm of the World Bank charged with providing an "objective assessment" of World Bank investments and drawing lessons for future projects, reviewed the project and gave it an overall rating of "unsatisfactory" (Independent Evaluation Group 2009). The rating reflected what the IEG called a "lack of government commitment and follow-through," especially in terms of investing oil revenues according to the World Bank's formula (2009, 38). But the IEG gave much higher marks to other components of the project. The group described the pipeline project as a "physical, technical, and financial success" (2009, xv). Despite Chad's "challenged crude," annual revenues to the government exceeded initial projections due to higher-than-expected oil prices.[2] The IEG also praised the project's use of specific governance mechanisms, including the *Environmental Management Plan* (EMP) and the social and environmental risk mitigation policies; the use of two project monitoring bodies, the International Advisory Group (IAG) and the External Compliance Monitoring Group (ECMG); and the Collège de Contrôle et de Surveillance des Revenus Pétroliers, the revenue monitoring body that, according to the IEG, allowed the project to attain a level of revenue transparency "nearly unique in Africa and nearing best international practice" (2009, 25).

While the IEG gave the project an overall rating of "unsatisfactory" because the government failed to adhere to the *Revenue Management Plan*, the IEG noted elsewhere in its report that the Chadian government had difficulty adhering to the

World Bank's formula for reasons that had nothing to do with corruption, mismanagement, or lack of "commitment" to the project's poverty reduction goals. The IEG judged, for instance, that the design of the plan was "prescriptive, overly detailed, and rigid" and that this led to "fragmentation of the budget, neglect of the quality of expenditure, and insufficient attention to budget execution" (2009, xiv). It also noted that the consortium moved far more quickly than anyone anticipated, and that the speed of the consortium's operations, including the fact that construction on the pipeline was completed one full year ahead of schedule (IAG 2009), confounded the government's efforts to create institutions capable of optimizing the use of oil revenues:

> The oil revenue accruing much sooner and in higher amounts than anticipated was a major factor underlying the program's failure to achieve its development objectives in Chad. The management arrangements devised for a comparatively limited amount of oil revenue cracked under the weight of the much larger revenue that materialized. The larger revenue also generated temptations and competing claims that were in part associated with the re-emergence of political instability and violent rebellion. The slow efforts at capacity building were undercut by the more rapid inflow of oil money. And the oil revenue much greater than the total of foreign aid sharply altered the initial leverage calculus of the program. (Independent Evaluation Group 2009, xiii)

While the IEG observed that the government's capacity-building efforts were undercut by the "rapid inflow of money," and that the systems the government put in place "cracked under the weight" of the larger-than-expected volume of oil money, it never connected the difficulties the government experienced with the model it was assessing.

Neither did the IAG, the World Bank–sponsored body charged with monitoring project implementation from 2001 until the bank withdrew from the project in 2008. Early in the project, the IAG identified what it called the "two-speed" problem of the consortium moving ahead at a rapid clip on the construction of the pipeline while the government's institutional capacity-building efforts lagged behind. The IAG treated the pace of the government's and the consortium's activities as inherent to them and as extrinsic to and entirely separate from the model whose implementation they were assigned to monitor:

> First of all, the "two-speed" problem cannot be disguised. What was at first a handicap is developing into a constraint, indeed a given: to the States' lack of readiness at the start of the process, we must now

add the cumbersome nature of procedures and the slow pace of actions by the governments and the World Bank as project execution
progresses. The commercial project is moving forward while the institutions are limping along: this places a dangerous handicap on the
hopes of achieving a true development project. (IAG 2001b, 11)

The recommendations the IAG offered as a means of addressing the two-speed
problem maintained the fiction that corporate efficiency was natural—it was just
corporate efficiency—and had nothing to do with the model itself. The IAG urged
the World Bank and the International Finance Corporation to assist the government and civil society groups in Chad to "do better and faster" (IAG 2002b, 18), and
it provided a continuous stream of tedious management advice to the government of Chad. At its first mention of the two-speed problem, for example, the IAG
wrote, "It may sometimes be useful to disengage projects with multiple components in order to avoid delays in one from impacting the whole" and "If necessary,
carry out a new comprehensive review of all these initiatives, assign priorities and
review the possibility of structural modifications or other changes to facilitate
their implementation" (IAG 2001a, 6). In subsequent reports the advice became
more pointed. In late 2001 the group wrote, "A demonstrated will to act is now
required" (IAG 2001b, 11), and six months later, "There is still enough time to take
the necessary actions and to focus on important strategic objectives that are still
achievable; what must not be done is to accept that the state of preparedness for
the arrival of oil revenues 'will be whatever it will be' " (IAG 2002b, 2). Yet in its
ongoing commentary on the two-speed regime, the IAG never shifted its focus from
the government to the consortium or asked how the consortium was able to work
with such ease and speed. What conditions allowed oil production to proceed not
on pace, but well ahead of it?

Corporate efficiency and the fact that oil revenues accrued "much sooner . . .
than anticipated" was the product of *work*, including efforts the consortium made
to separate itself from the farmers I followed. The deftness of the consortium was
a by-product of its deployment of anthropological claims about the oil field region
and the work it did to restrict its ongoing obligations to residents and to devolve
responsibility for a range of social projects to others—especially to farmers.

The consortium constructed fallowed land as "bush," making it available
for the taking, and farmers as individual users of state land who could be moved
off their plots because they "have other land they can easily put into cultivation"
(EEPCI 1999b, vol. 3, Appendix B). Farmers could be expected to self-resettle and
not need the assistance of the consortium because "it is so easy to re-establish
oneself" (EEPCI 1999b, vol. 3, sec. 6.8). The consortium presented the compensation and resettlement programs as comprising choices that people themselves

identified in participatory consultation sessions led by the consortium's staff anthropologist, who was linguistically competent, sensitive to local culture, and attuned to indigenous political processes. Farmers received guidance from consortium staff in making choices about compensation and resettlement, but they were accountable for their choices and the outcomes that followed, and they were left to sink or swim.

People in canton Miandoum divided up their land and compensation payments, managed the disputes that ensued in families, self-resettled, and rehabilitated themselves after the loss of land. Residents made their complaints legible to the consortium, and, with the help of intermediaries, turned them into problems the consortium could manage at a distance—through satellite offices and LCCs in villages far from the base camps—so the work of extraction could continue unimpeded. Occasionally they managed to sabotage the consortium's efforts to speed along, such as when they provoked a public relations crisis by becoming eligible for resettlement in record numbers, but these occasions were rare.

Multiple forms of work and of distancing and detachment were vital to the smooth implementation of the project and were entangled in the production of the resource curse. Struggles over how to live in the time of oil—what Candace Vogler (2002) calls "complex scenes"—played out in villages, families, and houses, but not at the gates of the base camps, along the pipeline, or at construction sites. The LCCs, community consultation sessions, reading rooms, satellite offices, blue binders, and waste dumps brought the project to people while simultaneously containing people in their villages and communities, away from the base camps and work sites. The domestication of disputes also reflected the ability of the consortium to cordon itself off from the villages of the canton through the establishment of a vast security apparatus and curfews, patrols, raids, checkpoints, travel authorizations, and house-to-house searches. These "harder" governance mechanisms operated in the background of the standards regime. They received far less press coverage than the EMP and were ignored by the IEG in its assessment of the overall model.

The consortium demanded that the state take an active role in maintaining order in the oil field region, and the consortium's policies were always backed up by force or the threat of it. Under its agreement with the consortium the Chadian state was contractually obligated to make it illegal "for any person to undertake activities which may interfere with the construction, operation and maintenance of the TOTCO [Tchad Oil Transportation Company] Transportation System"— effectively the pipeline and the broader project (Amnesty International 2005, 25). In expressing its objection to this clause, Amnesty International held it up as an example of preventing local populations, including workers, from demanding their rights. In part because of these kinds of clauses, which are designed to "create a stable and predictable environment for foreign investment" (Friends of the Earth, n.d., 7), repression is a signature mode of operating in the extractive industries:

> Stabilization clauses can also preclude or discourage governments from acting on their obligations to protect human rights, for example, by prohibiting actions that could slow or stop a project, such as respecting the workers' right to strike. One form of a stabilization clause, called an "equilibrium clause," mandates that the host government must financially compensate the company if any new social or environmental policy is enacted, or if a government takes action to meet human rights obligations, and this policy or action alters a project's financial balance. As a consequence, these investment contracts are public policy-setting documents. (Friends of the Earth, n.d., 7)

In the oil field region, land transfers and compensation payments were carried out in the shadow of a vast police and security presence. The consortium's community recycling program turned people and their homes and villages into sites of surveillance and unannounced raids and searches, and it kept people off roadways and away from installations, where they might be stopped and searched. Even community consultation sessions, which were supposed to engage residents in the planning of their own resettlement, involved the participation of armed police, lending the sessions an air of menace, intimidation, and coercion.

The consortium streamlined its operations in the oil field region by constructing person-land relations in ways that limited the need to enter into binding relationships with residents and by off-loading obligations and responsibilities for social projects onto others. The presence of the state in its security and administrative functions cleared the way for the consortium to operate unfettered by the demands of disgruntled workers or angry residents. As a result, the government's coffers were prematurely flooded with oil money, overrunning its efforts to build institutional capacity and effectively manage oil revenues for poverty reduction. The model did not prevent the resource curse; it helped to produce it.

Footprints

After the World Bank's withdrawal in 2008, the consortium continued to take and return land and to produce reports about the project. The production of progress reports dropped in frequency; the consortium transitioned from producing quarterly reports to semiannual, and then to annual reporting—but as of early 2015, the consortium continued to publish quarterly *LUMAP* reports and to post them to its website for the project. The *LUMAP* reports provide exceptionally detailed accounts of the consortium's patterns of land use in the oil field region and are part of its effort to demonstrate its ongoing commitment to the standards regime.

The *LUMAP* reports suggest that the consortium equated the extent and depth of the project's impact on local populations with the surface area the project covers. The consortium refers to both, conjointly, as the "project footprint." The consortium measured its impact on the communities of the oil field region through the metaphor of the footprint. The calculations of the project footprint were central to the consortium's efforts to document and report the impacts of its actions. In project documents, including reports by World Bank consultants and monitoring bodies, project land requirements became synonymous with the project's impact in the oil field region, as in: "This program [the in-fill drilling program] will increase the number of wells by up to 400, thereby increasing the overall size of the project's footprint, which was not foreseen in the original Environmental Impact Assessment" (IEG 2009, 34). Operators of resource extraction projects in Africa and elsewhere claim they can reduce their impacts on local settings by reducing their need for land. Extractive industry projects can be inserted into fragile ecologies and inhabited spaces while causing minimal harm or disruption because of the technological advances, smart design, and engineering prowess that allow them to reduce their size (Sawyer 2004). Smaller projects equal less disruptive projects.

Throughout the project, the consortium used the metaphor of the footprint to describe the effects of land expropriation as temporary and reversible. Take the construction of the pipeline, for example. To lay the pipeline, the consortium needed a thirty-meter-wide easement or "construction corridor." This land was supposed to be returned to farmers "shortly after the trench is backfilled" (EEPCI 1999b, vol. 3, sec. 3.3). Once the land was returned to farmers, they could use half of it with no restrictions while the half directly on top of the buried pipeline could be used to grow crops and graze animals, though not to build houses, plant trees, or conduct activities that would interfere with regular pipeline maintenance. The pipeline was supposed to be built in a single dry season, during a lull in the agricultural cycle. It was also supposed to be built in segments to minimize disruption at sites along the route, with each segment expected to take thirty to sixty days to complete—"the time required to clear the land; excavate the trench; lay, weld, and inspect the pipe; and backfill the trench" (EEPCI 1999b, vol. 3, sec. 3.3).

The consortium argued that project land needs *and* the impact of the project were minimized by building the pipeline underground, re-engineering existing well pads to reduce their size by 30 to 50 percent, locating new installations on already-acquired land, and, most importantly, instituting a land reclamation and return program, in which land that was no longer needed for the project was returned to farmers—an activity that predominated in the post-construction and post–World Bank years of the project. As part of this program, the consortium returned land to farmers that had been acquired for temporary use, including land needed for borrow pits, supply yards, and easements for high voltage power lines and flow lines. It also returned land that could be reclaimed by reducing the size of existing installations post-construction. To make reclaimed land suitable for farming again, the consortium loosened compacted soil in a process it referred to as "scarification" and applied a layer of topsoil. The consortium then released the land back to communities in formal ceremonies where restrictions on land use, such as prohibitions against lighting fires, planting trees, or building structures, were explained to farmers[3] (EEPCI 2005b, 38, 41). The World Bank described the land reclamation and return program as an example of "project footprint reinstatement" (IFC 2006, 8). At various stages in the project the consortium, the World Bank, and the World Bank's monitoring bodies described project footprint as "shrinking" (EEPCI 2003, 23), as "significantly reduced" (IEG 2009, 34), and as "its lowest in years" (EEPCI 2012, 55).

The metaphor of the footprint and the emphasis on technologies to miniaturize installations and shrink and contain the project gave way to a flood of numbers about the amount of land the consortium needed, took, held, and returned. The consortium's quarterly *LUMAP* reports contain color-coded bar graphs that chart fluctuations over time in the project's footprint. The graphs are accompanied by tables displaying the number of hectares acquired for permanent facilities and the number temporarily occupied by the consortium, as well as how much of the land under temporary occupation has been returned to farmers and is available to them with and without land use restrictions. The figures on land occupation are also presented by village. Villages in the oil field region are ordered into four categories—"low," "moderate," "approaching high," and "high" impact—that are supposed to reflect the scope of the project footprint and therefore the severity of the project's impact on them.

The emphasis in the *LUMAP* reports is not on the overall amount of land occupied by the consortium, but on the dynamic nature of the consortium's land needs, and especially on the consortium's gradual but inexorable retreat in the waning years of the project. In each quarter, villages can shift status and can move up or down the rankings as portions of the village land base are taken or returned. By returning land to farmers the consortium could not only minimize the project's footprint, it could also erase it. The graphs in the *LUMAP* reports document the consortium's territorial retreat and foretell a future like the one Barry (2013) describes for the communities around the Baku-Tibilisi-Ceyhan pipeline, in which the *LUMAP* reports with their records of expropriation and return will be, by this telling, the only remaining artifact of the project.

The Raw Material of Policy

Like the World Bank's postmortem for the pipeline, most of the writing on the project has focused on the *Revenue Management Plan* and on the government's use of oil revenues. The World Bank, nongovernmental organizations (NGOS), journalists, and academics have described the plan as a "novel" institutional arrangement and have followed its implementation closely (Independent Evaluation Group 2009; Gary and Karl 2003; Leibold 2011). They have scrutinized the alignment of the government's allocation of oil revenues with the World Bank's formula; the composition of the Collège de Contrôle et de Surveillance des Revenues Pétroliers, the body that followed the money; the legal loopholes in the arrangement the government might seek to exploit; and the relationships between natural resources, conflict, and poverty. Could oil revenues fuel poverty reduction? Would Chad be able to beat the "resource curse"?

The specter of the resource curse haunted this project. It also haunts the study of extractive industry projects in general, obscuring the role of companies in the dynamics of enclave extraction (Watts 2004a). In recent years anthropologists and others have begun paying attention to aspects of corporate and transnational governance in the extractive sector (Appel 2012; Barry 2004, 2013; Couman 2011; Dolan and Rajak 2011; Gilberthorpe 2013; Li 2009, 2015; Welker, Partridge, and Hardin 2011; Zalik 2004), and this book contributes to that effort. Esso and the consortium of global oil companies it headed were at the center of this account, even as they remained diffident interlocutors for me and for residents of canton Miandoum.

I wrote this book to tell a story of the pipeline project that I thought at the outset had nothing to do with the macroeconomics of oil production, the resource curse, or the *Revenue Management Plan*. The debates that raged in the capital over the allocation of oil revenues echoed only faintly in the oil field region and not at all in the villages that were the focus of my fieldwork. People in the families I followed were much more concerned about the loss of their land, the lack of jobs, and the physical presence of oil installations in their lives than they were about government budgets and spending priorities. It was clear from the start of the project that the loss of land—what the consortium called the project footprint— would be a critical impact of the pipeline project, especially for families in canton Miandoum, where land pressure had been a source of concern before Conoco drilled its first successful test well in the 1970s. But the precipitous decline in the available land base, which was much more pronounced than anyone anticipated due to a dramatic expansion of the project in response to Chad's "challenged crude" and the consortium's lower-than-expected production figures, was not the only legacy of the project in the villages of the canton. What I found myself tracking were the effects of the model that have been glossed or ignored in postproject analyses and assessments—effects that turned out to be intertwined with events in N'Djamena and the demise of the project as an experiment in development.

The model of corporate and transnational governance that structured the Chad pipeline project shaped the lives of farmers who could not be physically removed. The *EMP* and the consortium's social and environmental risk mitigation policies created new categories of people and made new forms of relational subjectivity possible. The scramble for land separated family members who could clear land and put it into cultivation from those who could not. Farmers who could transform land into a "field" and who could figure out what to say to the consortium's agents about their families and their landholdings became eligible for compensation payments and resettlement benefits while others, "dependents" and *les non-éligibles,* did not. Gender was a critical axis of difference: women's access to land receded dramatically during the project and the compensation and resettlement policies increased women's dependency on men at a time when women's contributions to household economies were critical to food security and financial solvency. Ideas about relatedness and belonging lost their elasticity; groups of people with attachments elsewhere, outside the village, came to be defined as outsiders whose loyalty to the extended family was uncertain. The policies strained relational ties, but they also strengthened them, as families worked to shore up social networks and repair frayed alliances by recognizing and responding to claims to relatedness and by tracing family histories through the land. Social ties were refracted and transformed through the prism of the consortium's policies, but the policies also made new forms of connection and interaction possible.

The consortium's policies were performative in the sense that they created the behaviors they described (Shore and Wright 2011). But people also experienced self-government as oppressive and not necessarily as gaining agency or as liberating (Shore and Wright 1997). Farmers who became eligible for resettlement worked to demonstrate their ongoing commitment to rehabilitation and their desire for additional training and resources, but they resented the need to be always prepared for unannounced spot checks and monitoring visits. In response to the ubiquitous presence of security forces and the raids, patrols, and checkpoints, people changed their routes to steer clear of project installations and infrastructure, but they disliked having to deliberate about where to walk and what to carry. They were angered about the power of discarded objects to define them, the damage to their property, and the intrusion into their houses and lives on the part of security forces tasked with searching for the consortium's property. Families took up the task of allocating compensation payments and managing the disputes that ensued from the layering of affective claims, but they objected to the consortium's rules governing compensation and resettlement, and perceived them as deeply unjust. Farmers wrote letters reciting the consortium's policies and asking the consortium to abide by them even when they expected no reply.

The work farmers and their families did was invisible in project documents; it happened entirely outside the texts and frameworks project monitors used, yet it facilitated the implementation of the project and allowed the consortium to build a pipeline in record time.

Postmortem for a Model

Despite what it called the project's "disappointing development outcome," the IEG concluded that the World Bank should continue to make "appropriate" investments in extractive industry projects (2009, v). For justification, the group provided a counterfactual claim. According to the IEG, the project in Chad resulted in stronger social and environmental protections and higher allocations of oil money to priority sectors of the economy than would otherwise have been the case.

The IEG's assessments are particularly interesting in light of the fact that development outcomes were never actually monitored as part of the project (Independent Evaluation Group 2009, xx). Ironically, the project that was supposed to serve as a model for all other extractive industry-as-development projects did not measure development or poverty reduction. The World Bank and the monitoring and oversight bodies it sponsored tracked government investments of oil revenues in key sectors of the economy, but made no effort to look at what those investments did or did not accomplish. The IEG recognized this monitoring gap and described it as "a serious shortcoming for a program whose main objective was poverty reduction through the use of oil revenue" (2009, xiii). It chided the World Bank for its flawed formulation of the project's development goals, writing,

> Clearly, production and export of oil are not, *in themselves,* development objectives. Indeed, the term "thereby" implies that the objective was to increase fiscal revenues (for Cameroon) and expenditures for poverty reduction (for Chad). But even that objective was inappropriately phrased for Chad, on two counts. First, the objective is defined in terms of inputs, and it cannot be a *development* objective to spend more on one activity or another. Worse, defining the objective as "increasing expenditures" can be misinterpreted as an open invitation to loosen expenditure controls and / or engage in wasteful expenditure— as demonstrated by the experience with the typical recommendations of the Public Expenditure Reviews of the 1980s. It is surprising to still find that approach at work in 1999, when the need for some orientation

toward the *results* of public spending was already well understood at
the Bank. (2009, 11)

If the role of the World Bank was to be the "moral guarantor" for the project
(Darrow 2003), then who or what did it underwrite? The bank imposed the *Revenue
Management Plan* on the government of Chad and provided monitoring and super-
visory oversight for the project. World Bank–sponsored monitoring and oversight
bodies adopted the consortium's framework as their starting and ending points;
the IAG called the EMP the "enforcement document on environmental and social
issues for the entire duration of the Project" (IAG 2004, 2). The World Bank, the
IAG, and the External Compliance Monitoring Group (ECMG) backed the consortium's model of corporate governance, reinforcing it, lending it legitimacy, and
doing the work of the consortium in showing the consortium to be adhering to a
transnational standards regime or at least committed to such a regime.

The internal contradictions in World Bank–sponsored evaluations and monitoring reports were frequent and stark, but they were also ignored or glossed over,
suggesting that ideological faith in the power of the model or in abstract moral
virtues like perseverance (Guyer 2011) kept the project moving forward. Robert
Barclay and George Koppert found that the on- and off-farm training programs
were utter failures, but they also reported—quite distinctly, though in the same
report—that the households of farmers who were enrolled in the training programs were better off than others. The IAG commented repeatedly in its trip reports about the "two-speed problem," but it interrogated the reasons for only one
speed, that of the government—never asking how the consortium managed to
move so quickly, and never connecting the consortium's speed with the implementation of the model it was tracking. The IAG's mandate was to advise the World
Bank and the governments of Chad and Cameroon "about overall progress in
implementation of the Projects and in achievement of their social, environmental,
and poverty alleviation objectives as well as with the broader goals of poverty
alleviation and sustainable development in Chad and Cameroon" (World Bank
2001), yet the IAG failed to notice that no poverty alleviation outcomes had been
identified.

The IEG had its own blind spots. It noted that the speed and scale of oil revenues overran the government's efforts to build institutions and manage the funds
for poverty reduction, yet the lessons it drew from this experiment focused only
on the failings of the government, including its lack of "commitment and follow
through" (IEG 2009, 38). These blind spots made it possible for the IEG to urge the
World Bank not to "avoid appropriate involvement in extractive industries" but
instead to invest in these projects "mindful of the important lessons of this complex experience" (2009, v).

The legacy of the pipeline project for people in the oil field region will not only be determined by the failure of the Chadian government to invest oil revenues in critical sectors of the economy or by the footprint of the consortium and the amount of land given over to permanent facilities in the region. The imprint of the project will not recede or disappear even when the last bits of land are returned to people in 2025 or when the project ends and the oil fields run dry. Like the imposition of mandatory cotton cultivation in *le Tchad utile* in the colonial period, the last major attempt to render southern Chad useful, the future of the region—in its ecology and its modes of social organization—will be forever marked by oil and by a consortium of global oil companies who turned life upside down while working feverishly to leave no footprint behind.

NOTES

1. An Experiment in Development

The original French version of this chapter's epigraph reads, "'Tout le pays a les yeux tournées vers la région de Doba qui est devenue le centre de l'attention nationale avec les activités de CONOCO. Certes, trouver du pétrole est toujours un jeu de dés. Mais quand les efforts de cette société seront couronnés de succès, des industries supportant des installations complexes et spécialisées surgiront par voies de conséquence. La clef du problème que pose le développement sera trouvé, et nous serons alors en mesure de redonner a tout le Tchad une dimension objective" (my translation).

1. Throughout the book I use pseudonyms for members of the households I followed and for residents of the oil field region.

2. Conoco struck oil in October of 1974; Tombalbaye was assassinated on April 13, 1975.

3. The term *model* has been used in connection with other oil and pipeline projects. For instance, Andrew Barry notes that BP described the Baku-Tbilisi-Ceyhan (BTC) pipeline as "a new model for large-scale, extractive-industry investments by major, multinational enterprises in developing and transition countries" (2013, 4).

4. Chad has been wracked by a series of internal conflicts that began in 1965 (see Buijtenhuijs 1987 and Gatta 2001). As Debos (2013) has shown, violence has also become a mode of governing even in the inter-war years.

5. There is a vast literature on the resource curse. Some analyses that discuss general trends, are not country specific, and are representative of the resource curse thesis include Auty (1993); Collier and Hoeffler (2005); Karl (1997); Ross (1999); Sachs and Warner (1995); and van der Ploeg (2006). Botswana is sometimes cited as an African exception to the resource curse. On this point see van der Ploeg (2006).

6. In fact, 80 percent of royalties and 85 percent of dividends were to be allocated to priority sectors of the economy. An additional 15 percent of royalties and 15 percent of dividends were to be deposited in a "special treasury account" in a commercial bank until 2007, after which these revenues were also to be allocated to priority sectors of the economy; for a schematic representation of the *Revenue Management Plan,* see Gary and Karl 2003.

7. The inability of people to tell "who is doing what" (Barry 2004) extends to the authorship of the EMP. The document appears to be an anonymously authored consensus document—a statement of official policy—and not a document that embeds a set of political

or ideological principles in the operations of the project (Shore and Wright 1997). A note in Volume 1 of the *EMP* indicates that Exxon Production Research in Houston, Texas, was contracted to "oversee the development of Volume 1" and to "serve as the editor" of the entire *EMP* (EEPCI 1999b, vol. 1, sec. 1.4). A list of fifty "contributors" to volume 1 includes individuals from Exxon Production Research in Houston, Texas; the government of Chad; Esso Exploration and Production Chad, Inc.; the Tchad Oil Transportation Company; Imperial Oil Resources Limited in Alberta, Canada; Dames & Moore; and "independent socioeconomic consultants" (EEPCI 1999b, vol. 1, sec. 8.0). But no list of contributors or authorship credits is provided for the other five volumes of the *EMP*.

8. See also Shever (2012).

9. The maps are proprietary and cannot be reprinted, but they can be accessed at ExxonMobil's website for the Chad/Cameroon Pipeline Project (http://www.essochad .com/Chad-English/PA/Operations/TD_ProjectMaps.aspx) and can be found in volume 3 of the *EMP*, the *Compensation and Resettlement Plan*.

10. The consortium justified the structure of the compensation and resettlement scheme and described that scheme as evidence of "sensitivity to cultural practices and local legal requirements" by describing land tenure practices in Chad this way: "In Chad and Cameroon, nearly all land is legally owned by the state. So farmers, rather than owning land as in Europe or North America, have only the use of the land for crops. The project therefore does not buy land but compensates for farmer labor and lost crop opportunities as provided in the *EMP*" (EEPCI 2006, 36).

2. Dead Letters

1. Esso is the name of ExxonMobil's operating company in Chad.

2. Grievance mechanisms are required under the latest version of the standard on involuntary resettlement, Operational Policy (OP) 4.12, for category A projects, which the World Bank defines as projects that are "likely to have significant adverse environmental impacts that are sensitive, diverse, or unprecedented."

3. Locals referred to the settlement as Attend because it was a place where people went to wait—*attend*—in the hope of getting work with the consortium, or sometimes they referred to it as Satan, because bars and prostitutes were ubiquitous. The consortium took an active role in cleaning up the settlement and in renaming the village by making road signs that read "Atan" (a word that is neither French nor Ngambaye) and "Atan Village."

4. The person who received grievances on behalf of the consortium is described in the *Compensation and Resettlement Plan* as the EDR, or the Esso designated representative. In Chad, the EDRs were the LCCs.

5. This is what the consortium said about paying compensation to people who farmed land where the consortium had already placed its surveyors' stakes:

> With one important exception, all fields and all buildings and structures composing the homestead will be compensated for as outlined in the following sections. **Compensation will <u>not</u> be made for any building or field created on a piece of land after notification of its use by the Project has already**

been given. Anyone who builds on, or farms, this land after notification will do so at the risk of losing their investment. (EEPCI 1999b, vol. 3, sec. 5.1; emphasis in the original)

6. It was common knowledge that people paid the LCCs to get jobs with the consortium. However, members of the World Bank's evaluation teams either dismissed residents' reports as "sour grapes" or transposed their claims to suggest that if corruption occurred it was local authorities who had been corrupted and not consortium employees, as in this excerpt from a monitoring report:

> Some villagers, probably those that were unlucky, allege that the lists of workers supplied by the village chiefs were designed so that the chiefs' favorites were recruited first and that the last few vacant places were filled by the lottery in order "to save face." "If Esso needs ten workers, the Chef de Canton and Esso's LCC will first share the number and each will have three. In the end, only the last four places will be drawn from the population by lottery." In fact, the lottery system was instituted . . . by an idea voiced among the population during public consultations in response to the major concern that all candidates should have equal access to the available jobs. This did not mean that some candidates did not try to increase their chances by proposing money to the canton or village chief assuming that despite the lottery system, they would get priority. (Cogels and Koppert 2004, 32)

7. All letters used in this chapter are my translations.

8. MWIL stands for Miandoum Water Injection Line. I altered the specific location of the land in question so the letter writer could not be identified.

9. In one of its reports, the World Bank's International Advisory Group wrote, "The accessibility of project documentation to all interested parties remains inequitable. The Consortium is making documents available to university researchers, but local NGOs are complaining that not all of the basic documentation on environmental issues is accessible to them" (IAG 2001, 5). This did not reflect my experience with the consortium. In more than twelve years of fieldwork I never received complaint data or any other documentation from the consortium other than a CD copy of the *Environmental Management Plan,* a document that is publicly available online. Journalists, including Stephanie Braquehais of Radio France Internationale, described similar difficulties in obtaining access to information and to the consortium's camps and work sites, as well as restrictions the consortium placed on photography; see Braquehais (2009).

10. I am indebted to Anatoli Ignatov for bringing the parallels to my attention and for giving me a copy of Kafka's novel.

3. Becoming "Eligible"

1. There is a separate *EMP* for Cameroon, which also comprises six volumes.

2. The World Bank uses the term *resettlement* to refer to the displacement—physical and otherwise—of people, as well as the remedial measures put in place to mitigate the

effects of displacement (World Bank 2004). In the voluminous literature on involuntary resettlement, the terms *resettlement, involuntary resettlement, forced displacement,* and *development-induced displacement* are often used interchangeably. General volumes on the topic include Cernea and Mathur 2008; Mehta 2009; Modi 2009; and Oliver-Smith 2009.

3. Expatriate employees posted photographs and comments about the camps and work life on social media outlets, and their postings were more informative about life inside the camps than were any of the consortium's publications. See, for example, the photos and comments posted by Ken Doerr on flickr.com (https://www.flickr.com/photos/ken doerr/8079983452/in/photostream/). These unofficial postings often presented aspects of the project that were not otherwise available to the public, including comments about working conditions, problems with project infrastructure, and oil spills. Doerr's photographic essay includes a picture of the "pipeline trench team" with the caption, "84 guys, 42 picks and 42 shovels. 40 deg C heat. Long days." Another photograph of the same pipeline trench team is captioned, "The 1100km export line to an fso [Floating storage and off loading vessel] off Cameroon is in need of some TLC. 6000 field welds are suffering from corrosion and need to be carefully excavated by hand to avoid any damage. A fibre-optic line is buried in the same trench." Doerr also captured a "flowline leak" that, he estimates, led to a spill of half a barrel of oil.

4. Community compensation was allocated to villages for the loss of land the consortium referred to as "bush." Villages were asked to choose one form of compensation from a menu of options that included one kilometer of paved road, a well, two schoolrooms, and market stalls. Later in the project, villages designated as being subjected to high impact from the project received an additional item from the same menu of options.

5. The rural oil field region in Chad is populated by the Ngambaye and is not ethnically or culturally diverse. However, the pipeline spans over one thousand kilometers, and there is considerable ethnic and cultural diversity along its route.

6. See Chad/Cameroon Development Project, "Consultation," http://www.exxonmobil.com/Chad/Library/Photo_Video/web_photoalbum/english/04b.html.

7. The consortium does not cite any studies to support its claim that self-resettlement leads to higher rates of success than resettlement efforts that are managed by governments or other agencies. The consensus view in the literature is that the World Bank's record with involuntary resettlement "is one of dismal failure" (Clark 2009, 196; see also Cernea and Mathur 2008), but to my knowledge there are no published studies of self-resettlement, which seems to be a mutation and innovation of this particular project.

8. For example, the evaluation team that reported the systemic failures of the training programs suggested that they did not work because farmers were irresponsible or were poor money managers (Barclay and Koppert 2007), and the iag suggested that farmers used resources in nonsustainable ways because they lacked information and awareness (iag 2009).

9. The consortium described the formula used to calculate eligibility for resettlement as follows: "An individual who has access to less than 2/3 corde of land (both cultivated and fallow), for each person s/he declares as a member of his or her household, is eligible for resettlement" (eepci 1999b, vol. 3, app. B).

10. The *corde* is a unit of land, equivalent to roughly half a hectare, that takes its name from the overseer's cord (in French, *corde*) that was used to measure the plots farmers were mandated to clear and put into cultivation.

11. The struggles are also disconnected from changes in the World Bank's policies on involuntary resettlement. Cernea and his colleagues created the bank's first policy on involuntary resettlement in 1980. This policy was known as Operational Manual Statement (OMS) 2.33 and titled "Social Issues Associated with Involuntary Resettlement in Bank Financed Projects." It was written as a "statement" for the bank's operational manual, and it was intended "for the guidance of staff at the World Bank" (World Bank 1980). A series of revisions to it in 1986, 1988, and 1990 added new elements to the policy and made it more precise (Clark 2009; Davis 2004; Park 2010). OMS 2.33 was amended in 1986 as OMS 10.08, "Operations Issues in the Treatment of Involuntary Resettlement in Bank Financed Projects." The 1990 version of the policy, known as Operational Directive (OD) 4.30, succeeded OMS 10.08 and reflected the emergence of a consensus inside the World Bank about how to execute involuntary resettlement programs (Clark 2009; Shihata 2000; World Bank 2004). Critical components of OD 4.30 included the idea that physical resettlement should be avoided whenever possible and should be considered a strategy of last resort; that resettlement projects should function as development projects and should improve or at least restore the living standards of the people who are displaced; and that community participation in the design and implementation of resettlement programs should be encouraged. In 1997, this standard on involuntary resettlement became one of the World Bank's "safeguard policies"—a suite of social and environmental policies that are compulsory elements of certain bank-sponsored projects, including the pipeline project in Chad.

4. Ties That Bind

1. On the difficulties of obtaining private title to land in sub-Saharan Africa, see Njoh (1998), who describes the process for Cameroon.

2. The International Advisory Group (IAG), one of the World Bank's monitoring bodies, frequently described the project as having a "two-speed" problem (IAG 2001, 6). The IAG observed that the consortium moved much more quickly than did the government or NGOs, and it attributed this to "the discrepancy between their capacities" (2001, 3), but it did not note how families helped the consortium to expropriate their land—and to do it expeditiously—by reconfiguring their relational ties at the demand of the consortium and the state.

3. In-kind compensation was offered as an alternative to cash payments at the start of the project, but was phased out over time due to the lack of demand. People found the items the consortium offered expensive and of low quality. The delivery of items was often delayed, and the items received were not always the same as the ones featured in the consortium's catalog.

4. Ngambaye is the language spoken throughout the oil field region.

5. The plots were of varying shapes and sizes, and few of them were perfect seventy-meter-square *cordes*, but the number of plots in a category provides a rough proxy of the surface area farmed.

6. The consortium argued that researchers at the Centre de Coopération Internationale en Recherche Agronomique pour le Développement indicated that farmers who maintained a 1:1 ratio of land in cultivation to land in fallow were "barely maintaining soil fertility" (EEPCI 1999, vol. 3, app. B). I could not find anyone at the agricultural research station in the oil field region that concurred with that estimate. A soil scientist who participated on my research project estimated that a ratio of at least 1:3 would be needed to maintain soil fertility.

7. This count doesn't include plots women farmed outside the three villages, but this was likely to be offset by the reverse trend, or by women like Rodrique and Minga's daughter, who lived elsewhere but farmed family land in the three villages.

8. On gender and changing forms of kinship and person-land relations in the context of a differently structured oil project, see Gilberthorpe (2007).

9. The consortium recorded family members in their database as "dependents" for the purposes of determining whether the household remained economically viable or was eligible for resettlement, and whether the beneficiary of the compensation payment was also eligible to be enrolled in a training program. But dependents were not assumed to have shared claims to land.

5. In the Midst of Things

1. While the consortium tried to recruit community members to help it guard its installations, it did not enter into the kinds of relationships between oil companies and residents Adunbi (2011) describes in the Niger Delta, where families who had customary use rights over land on which oil installations were located become "host families" to the oil companies. Members of these families were paid by the oil companies to cut grass, and as "surveillance contractors" who protected the installations sited on their land from "intruders" and held keys to the fenced plots (2011, 107).

2. The IAG reported on various administrative glitches that led the consortium and its sub-contractors to bury useful objects: "Some of Esso's contractors, in rapid demobilization, did not receive authorization from the Government in time to give certain equipment to the local populations, and had to bury them. In addition, since Esso stopped its donation program for several weeks in order to adapt it to the ECMG group's recommendations and governmental requirements, it had to bury the waste that had accumulated during this time. The local populations watched in disbelief as useful equipment was buried, and, in some cases, they dug it back up later (IAG 2004, 18).

6. Footprints

1. On September 5, 2008, the government of Chad repaid $65.7 million in loans and credits to the World Bank (Independent Evaluation Group 2009). The International Finance Corporation (IFC) is still invested in the project through loans to the consortium. According to the IEG, the IFC continues to monitor the consortium's implementation of the social and environmental safeguards (Independent Evaluation Group 2009, xi).

2. Prices have since dropped, and at the time of this writing benchmark Brent crude had fallen below fifty dollars per barrel for the first time since 2009.

3. The consortium described its ability to return land to farmers in terms of its informal acquisition of land. Because the consortium never purchased land and instead only compensated farmers for their labor, it maintained that it was able to return the land to them more easily:

> In keeping with local land ownership and use concepts, the project did not
> buy title to the land as it might have done in a western country where most
> property is privately owned. Instead, in accordance with a process set out in
> the EMP, the project compensated farmers for their labor in clearing the land
> and planting crops. In this sense, the project compensates for land use but
> does not actually acquire the land. This approach makes it possible to return
> the land when work has been completed. (EEPCI 2005b, 41)

BIBLIOGRAPHY

Adunbi, O. (2011). Oil and the production of competing subjectivities in Nigeria. *African Studies Review, 54*(3), 101–120.

Ahmed, S. (2004). Affective economies. *Social Text, 22*(2), 117–139.

Alexander, C. (2005). Value: Economic valuations and environmental policy. In J. Carrier (Ed.), *A handbook of economic anthropology* (pp. 455–471). Cheltenham, England: Edward Elgar.

Amnesty International. (1997). *Extrajudicial executions: Fear for safety.* AFR 20/12/97. Author.

Amnesty International. (2005). *Contracting out of human rights: The Chad-Cameroon Pipeline Project.* London: Author.

Appadurai, A. (Ed.). (1986). *The social life of things: Commodities in cultural perspective.* Cambridge: Cambridge University Press.

Appel, H. (2012). Offshore work: Oil, modularity, and the how of capitalism in Equatorial Guinea. *American Ethnologist, 39*(4), 692–709.

Auty, R. M. (1993). *Sustaining development in mineral economies: The resource curse thesis.* London: Routledge.

Ballard, C. and Banks, G. (2003). Resource wars: The anthropology of mining. *Annual Review of Anthropology, 32,* 287–313.

Barclay, R., and Koppert, G. (2007, January). *Chad Resettlement and Compensation Plan evaluation study.* Paris: Group d'Etude des Populations Forestières Equatoriales.

Bardinet, C. (1977). Le canton de Goundi au Tchad en 1977: Etude de géographie économique. In *L'homme et le milieu: Aspects du développement au Tchad* (pp. 1–40). Paris: Institut de Géographie de l'Université Paris VIII.

Barry, A. (2004). Ethical capitalism. In W. Larner and W. Walters (Eds.), *Global governmentality: Governing international spaces* (pp. 195–211). London: Routledge.

Barry, A. (2006). Technological zones. *European Journal of Social Theory, 9,* 239–253.

Barry, A. (2013). *Material politics: Disputes along the pipeline.* Chichester: Wiley-Blackwell.

Berry, S. (1993). *No condition is permanent: The social dynamics of agrarian change in sub-Saharan Africa.* Madison: University of Wisconsin Press.

Braquehais, S. (2009). *Paris-N'Djamena, allers-retours.* Paris: L'Harmattan.

Buijtenhuijs, R. (1987). *Le Frolinat et les guerres civiles du Tchad (1977–1984).* Paris: Karthala.

Burchell, G. (1991). Peculiar interests: Civil society and governing "the system of natural liberty." In G. Burchell, C. Gordon, and P. Miller (Eds.), *The Foucault effect: Studies in governmentality* (pp. 119–150). Chicago: University of Chicago Press.

Cabot, J. (1955). La mise en valeur des régions du Moyen-Logone. *Annales de Géographie: Bulletin de la Société de Géographie, 64,* 35–46.

Cabot, J. (1961). Au Tchad, le problème des koros, Département du Logone. *Annales de Géographie: Bulletin de la Société de Géographie, 70,* 621–633.

Cabot, J. (1965). *Le basin du Moyen Logone.* Paris: Office de la Recherche Scientifique et Technique d'Outre-Mer.

Carrier, J. (1998). Property and social relations in Melanesian anthropology. In C. M. Hann (Ed.), *Property relations: Renewing the anthropological tradition* (pp. 85–103). Cambridge: Cambridge University Press.

Cernea, M. M. (1988). *Involuntary resettlement in development projects: Policy guidelines in World Bank–financed projects.* World Bank Technical Paper no. 80. Washington, DC: World Bank.

Cernea, M. M. (2008). Compensation and investment in resettlement: Theory, practice, pitfalls, and needed policy reform. In M. M. Cernea and H. M. Mathur (Eds.), *Can compensation prevent impoverishment? Reforming resettlement through investments and benefit-sharing* (pp. 15–98). New York: Oxford University Press.

Cernea, M. M., and Mathur, H. M. (Eds.). (2008). *Can compensation prevent impoverishment? Reforming resettlement through investments and benefit-sharing.* New York: Oxford University Press.

Certeau, M. de (2002). *The practice of everyday life* (Steven F. Rendall, Trans.). Berkeley: University of California Press.

Clark, D. (2009). An overview of revisions to the World Bank resettlement policy. In L. Mehta (Ed.), *Displaced by development: Confronting marginalization and gender injustice* (pp. 195–224). Los Angeles: Sage.

Cogels, S., and Koppert, G. (2004). *Socioeconomic monitoring survey in the Chad oil field development area and pipeline corridor.* Paris: Groupe d'Etude des Populations Forestières Equatoriales.

Coll, S. (2012). *Private empire: ExxonMobil and American power.* New York: Penguin.

Collier, P., and Hoeffler, A. (2005). Resource rents, governance, and conflict. *Journal of Conflict Resolution, 49,* 625–633.

Colloredo-Mansfeld, R. (2003). Matter unbound. *Journal of Material Culture, 8*(3), 245–254.

Comaroff, J. and Comaroff, J. (eds.). (2001). *Millennial capitalism and the culture of neoliberalism.* Durham: Duke University Press.

Compliance Advisor/Ombudsman. (2008). *A guide to designing and implementing grievance mechanisms for development projects.* Washington, DC: Office of the Compliance Advisor/Ombudsman.

CotonTchad. (2012). Country statement at the 71st plenary meeting of the International Cotton Advisory Committee, October 7–12, 2012. Author.

Coumans, C. (2011). Occupying spaces created by conflict: Anthropologists, development NGOs, responsible investment, and mining. *Current Anthropology, 52*(S3), S29–S43.

Craig, D., and Porter, D. (2006). *Development beyond neoliberalism: Governance, poverty reduction and political economy.* London: Routledge.

Cross, J. (2011). Detachment as a corporate ethic: Materializing CSR in the diamond
supply chain. *Focaal: Journal of Global and Historical Anthropology, 60,* 34–46.

Dames and Moore. (1997). *Chad Export Project: Environmental assessment.* Unpublished
manuscript.

Darrow, M. (2003). *Between light and shadow: The World Bank, the International Monetary
Fund, and international human rights law.* Oxford: Hart.

Das, V., and Poole, D. (2004). *Anthropology in the margins of the state.* Santa Fe, NM: School
of American Research Press.

Davis, G. (2004). *A history of the social development network in the World Bank, 1973–2002.*
Social Development Paper no. 56. Washington, DC: World Bank.

Dean, M. (1999). *Governmentality: Power and rule in modern society.* London: Sage.

Debos, M. (2013). *Le métier des armes au Tchad: Le gouvernment de l'entre-guerres.* Paris:
Karthala.

Dolan, C., and Johnstone-Louis, M. (2011). Re-siting corporate responsibility: The
making of South Africa's Avon entrepreneur. *Focaal: Journal of Global and Historical
Anthropology, 60,* 21–33.

Dolan, C., and Rajak, D. (2011). Introduction: Ethnographies of corporate ethicizing.
Focaal: Journal of Global and Historical Anthropology, 60, 3–8.

Douglas, M. (2002). *Purity and danger.* New York: Routledge.

Dwivedi, R. (2002). Models and methods in development-induced displacement.
Development and Change, 33(4), 709–732.

Edensor, T. (2005). Waste matter: The debris of industrial ruins and the disordering of the
material world. *Journal of Material Culture, 10*(3), 311–332.

Ellison, J. (2009). Governmentality and the family: Neoliberal choices and emergent kin
relations in southern Ethiopia. *American Anthropologist, 111*(1), 81–92.

Energy Sector Management Assistance Programme. (2005, October). *Crude oil price
differentials and differences in oil qualities: A statistical analysis.* ESMAP Technical Paper
081. Washington, DC: Author.

Esso Exploration and Production Chad, Inc. (EEPCI). (1999a). *Environmental assessment
executive summary and update.* Author. Retrieved from http://www.esso.com/Chad
-English/PA/Newsroom/TD_Documentation_Assessment.aspx.

Esso Exploration and Production Chad, Inc. (EEPCI). (1999b, May). *Environmental
management plan—Chad portion.* Author. Retrieved from http://www.esso.com
/Chad-English/PA/Newsroom/TD_Documentation_Chad.aspx.

Esso Exploration and Production Chad, Inc. (EEPCI). (2000). *Chad-Cameroon Development
Project, quarterly report no. 1, fourth quarter 2000.* Author. Retrieved from http://www
.esso.com/Chad-English/PA/Newsroom/TD_ProgressReports3.aspx.

Esso Exploration and Production Chad, Inc. (EEPCI). (2001). *Chad-Cameroon Development
Project, quarterly report no. 2, first quarter 2001.* Author. Retrieved from http://www
.esso.com/Chad-English/PA/Newsroom/TD_ProgressReports3.aspx

Esso Exploration and Production Chad, Inc. (EEPCI). (2003). *Chad-Cameroon Development
Project, project update no. 11, 2nd quarter 2003.* Author. Retrieved from http://www
.esso.com/Chad-English/PA/Newsroom/TD_ProgressReports3.aspx

Esso Exploration and Production Chad, Inc. (EEPCI). (2005a). *Chad-Cameroon Development Project, project update no. 19, annual report 2005.* Author. Retrieved from http://www .esso.com/Chad-English/PA/Newsroom/TD_ProgressReports3.aspx

Esso Exploration and Production Chad, Inc. (EEPCI). (2005b). *Chad Export Project: Project update no. 18, mid-year 2005.* Author. Retrieved from http://www.esso.com/Chad -English/PA/Newsroom/TD_ProgressReports3.aspx

Esso Exploration and Production Chad, Inc. (EEPCI). (2006). *Chad-Cameroon Development Project, project update no. 21, annual report 2006.* Author. Retrieved from http://www .esso.com/Chad-English/PA/Newsroom/TD_ProgressReports3.aspx

Esso Exploration and Production Chad, Inc. (EEPCI). (2008a). *Chad Export Project: Project update no. 24, mid-year report 2008.* Author. Retrieved from http://www.esso.com /Chad-English/PA/Newsroom/TD_ProgressReports3.aspx

Esso Exploration and Production Chad Inc. (EEPCI). (2008b, January). *Land use mitigation action plan: Annual individual livelihood restoration report 2007.* Author. Retrieved from http://www.esso.com/Chad-English/PA/Newsroom/TD_Documentation _Landuse.aspx

Esso Exploration and Production Chad Inc. (EEPCI). (2008c). *Land use mitigation action plan: Village impact quarterly report. Third quarter, 2008.* Author. Retrieved from http:// www.esso.com/Chad-English/PA/Newsroom/TD_Documentation_Landuse.aspx

Esso Exploration and Production Chad Inc. (EEPCI). (2009, February). *Land use mitigation action plan: Annual individual livelihood restoration report 2008.* Author. Retrieved from http://www.esso.com/Chad-English/PA/Newsroom/TD_Documentation _Landuse.aspx

Esso Exploration and Production Chad, Inc. (EEPCI). (2010). *Chad Export Project: Project update no. 29.* Author. Retrieved from http://www.esso.com/Chad-English/PA /Newsroom/TD_ProgressReports3.aspx

Esso Exploration and Production Chad, Inc. (EEPCI). (2011). *Chad-Cameroon Development Project, project update no. 31, year end report 2011.* Author. Retrieved from http://www .esso.com/Chad-English/PA/Newsroom/TD_ProgressReports3.aspx

Esso Exploration and Production Chad, Inc. (EEPCI). (2012). *Chad-Cameroon Development Project, project update no. 33, year-end report 2012.* Author. Retrieved from http://www .esso.com/Chad-English/PA/Newsroom/TD_ProgressReports3.aspx

Esso Exploration and Production Chad, Inc. (EEPCI). (2013, March). *Land use mitigation action plan: Annual individual livelihood restoration report 2012.* Author. Retrieved from http://www.esso.com/Chad-English/PA/Newsroom/TD_Documentation _Landuse.aspx

Esso Exploration and Production Chad, Inc. (EEPCI). (2014, October). *Land use mitigation action plan: Village impact quarterly report. Third quarter 2014.* Author. Retrieved from http://www.esso.com/Chad-English/PA/Newsroom/TD_Documentation _Landuse.aspx

External Compliance Monitoring Group (ECMG). (2003a, June). *Report of the External Compliance Monitoring Group: Chad Export Project. Eighth site visit, May 2003.* Genova, Italy: Author.

External Compliance Monitoring Group (ECMG). (2003b, December). *Report of the External Compliance Monitoring Group: Chad Export Project. Ninth site visit, October–November 2003.* Genova, Italy: Author.

External Compliance Monitoring Group (ECMG). (2004, June). *Report of the External Compliance Monitoring Group: Chad Export Project. Tenth site visit, April–May 2004.* Genova, Italy: Author.

External Compliance Monitoring Group (ECMG). (2005, December). *Report of the External Compliance Monitoring Group: Chad Export Project. Second site visit post-project completion, November 2005.* Genova, Italy: Author.

External Compliance Monitoring Group (ECMG). (2007, March). *Report of the External Compliance Monitoring Group: Chad Export Project. Third site visit post-project completion, February 2007.* Genova, Italy: Author.

External Compliance Monitoring Group (ECMG). (2009, May). *Report of the External Compliance Monitoring Group: Chad Export Project. Fifth post-project completion visit, April–May 2009.* Genova, Italy: Author.

External Compliance Monitoring Group (ECMG). (2012, December). *Chad Export Project. Site visit: November–December 2012.* Genova, Italy: Author.

Ferguson, J. (1994). *Anti-politics machine: Development, depoliticization, and bureaucratic power in Lesotho.* St. Paul: University of Minnesota Press.

Ferguson, J. (2005). Seeing like an oil company: Space, security, and global capital in neoliberal Africa. *American Anthropologist, 107*(3), 377–382.

Ferguson, J. (2006). *Global shadows: Africa in the neoliberal world order.* Durham, NC: Duke University Press.

Fessha, Y., and Kirkby, C. (2008). A critical survey of sub-national autonomy in African states. *Publius, 38*(2), 248–271.

Foucault, M. (1982). The subject and power (L. Sawyer, Trans.). In H. Dreyfus and P. Rabinow (Eds.), *Michel Foucault: Beyond structuralism and hermeneutics* (pp. 208–226). Brighton, England: Harvester.

Foucault, M. (1991). Governmentality (C. Gordon, Trans.). In G. Burchell, C. Gordon, and P. Miller (Eds.), *The Foucault effect: Studies in governmentality* (pp. 87–104). Chicago: University of Chicago Press.

Friends of the Earth. (n.d.). *Extractive sector projects financed by export credit agencies: The need for foreign investment contract and revenue reform.* Author. Retrieved from http://pacificenvironment.org/downloads/The%20Need%20for%20Foreign%20Investment%20Contract%20%20Revenue%20Reform%20at%20ECAs%20_final_.pdf

Frow, J. (2003). Invidious distinction: Waste, difference, and classy stuff. In G. Hawkins and S. Muecke (Eds.), *Culture and waste: The creation and destruction of value* (pp. 25–38). New York: Rowman and Littlefield.

Gary, I., and Karl, T. L. (2003). *Bottom of the barrel: Africa's oil boom and the poor.* Baltimore: Catholic Relief Services.

Gary, I., and Reisch, N. (2005). *Chad's oil: miracle or mirage? Following the money in Africa's newest petro-state.* Baltimore and Washington DC: Catholic Relief Services and Bank Information Center.

Gatta, G.N. (2001). *Tchad: Guerre civile et désagrégation de l'état*. Paris : Présence Africaine.

Geertz, C. (1983). *Local knowledge: The interpretation of cultures*. New York: Basic Books.

Gilberthorpe, E. (2007). Fasu solidarity: A case study of kin networks, land tenure, and oil extraction in Kutubu, Papua New Guinea. *American Anthropologist, 109*(1), 101–112.

Gilberthorpe, E. (2013). In the shadow of industry: A study of culturization in Papua New Guinea. *Journal of the Royal Anthropological Institute, 19*, 261–278.

Gilg, J. P. (1970). Culture commercial et discipline agraire: Dobadéné (Tchad). *Etudes Rurales, 37*(37–39), 173–197.

Gille, Z. (2007). *From the cult of waste to the trash heap of history: The politics of waste in socialist and post-socialist Hungary*. Bloomington: Indiana University Press.

Gold, R., and Gonzalez, A. (2011, February 16). Exxon struggles to find new oil. *Wall Street Journal*.

Groupe de Recherche Alternatives et de Monitoring du Projet Petrole Tchad-Cameroun (GRAMP-TC). (2011, October 10). *Complaint from local inhabitants and communities in the Chad project area to compliance advisor/ombudsperson of the International Finance Corporation (IFC) of the World Bank Group*. N'Djamena, Chad: Author.

Grovogui, S., and Leonard, L. (2007). Oiling tyranny? Neoliberalism and global governance in Chad. *Studies in Political Economy, 79*, 35–59.

Gupta, A., and Ferguson, J. (1992). Beyond "culture": Space, identity, and the politics of difference. *Cultural Anthropology, 7*(1), 6–23.

Guyer, J. I. (2002). Briefing: The Chad-Cameroon Petroleum and Pipeline Development Project. *African Affairs, 101*, 109–115.

Guyer, J. I. (2011). Blueprints, judgment, and perseverance in a corporate context. *Current Anthropology, 52*(S3), S17–S25.

Halperin, D. M. (2003). Out of Australia. In G. Hawkins and S. Muecke (Eds.), *Culture and waste: The creation and destruction of value* (pp. 1–8). New York: Rowman and Littlefield.

Hawkins, G., and Muecke, S. (Eds.). (2003). *Culture and waste: The creation and destruction of value*. New York: Rowman and Littlefield.

Hilson, G. (2012). Corporate social responsibility in the extractive industries: Experiences from developing countries. *Resources Policy, 37*, 131–137.

Hirschman, A. O. (1970). *Exit, voice and loyalty: Responses to decline in firms, organizations, and states*. Cambridge, MA: Harvard University Press.

Hunt, N. R. (1999). *A colonial lexicon: Of birth ritual, medicalization, and mobility in the Congo*. Durham, NC: Duke University Press.

Independent Evaluation Group (IEG). (2009, November 20). *Program performance assessment report*. Report no. 50315. Washington DC: World Bank Group.

Inkpen, A. and Moffett, M. H. (2011). *The oil and gas industry: Management, strategy and finance*. Tulsa: PennWell.

International Advisory Group (IAG). (2001a, September). *Report of mission to Cameroon and Chad, July 19–August 3, 2001*. Montreal: Author.

International Advisory Group (IAG). (2001b, December). *Report of mission to Cameroon and Chad, November 14–25, 2001*. Montreal: Author.

International Advisory Group (IAG). (2002a, December). *Report of visit to Cameroon and Chad: October 15 to November 4, 2002.* Montreal: Author.

International Advisory Group (IAG). (2002b, July). *Report of visit to Chad, June 3–17, 2002.* Montreal: Author.

International Advisory Group (IAG). (2003, June). *Report of visit to Chad and Cameroon: April 21 to May 10, 2003.* Montreal: Author.

International Advisory Group (IAG). (2004, February). *Report of visit to Chad, December 5 to 21, 2003.* Montreal: Author.

International Advisory Group (IAG). (2004, December). *Report of mission 8 to Chad, October 10 to 26, 2004.* Montreal: Author.

International Advisory Group (IAG). (2005a, July). *Report of mission 9 to Chad and Cameroon, May 15 to June 6, 2005.* Montreal: Author.

International Advisory Group (IAG). (2005b, November). *Report of mission 10 to Chad and Cameroon: September 25 to October 18, 2005.* Montreal: Author.

International Advisory Group (IAG). (2006, November). *Report of mission 11 to Chad: September 24 to October 14, 2006.* Montreal: Author.

International Advisory Group (IAG). (2008, January). *Report of mission 13 to Chad and Cameroon: November 11 to December 1, 2007.* Montreal: Author.

International Advisory Group (IAG). (2009, September). *Final report.* Montreal: Author.

International Finance Corporation (IFC). (2006, September). *Lessons of experience: External monitoring of the Chad-Cameroon pipeline project.* Washington, DC: World Bank Group.

Kafka, F. (2009). *The castle* (M. Harman, Trans.). Wordsworth Editions.

Karl, T. L. (1997). *Paradox of plenty: Oil booms and petro-states.* Berkeley: University of California Press.

Kelly, D. (2004, June 25). Doba finds a home. *International Oil Daily.*

Kopytoff, I. (1986). The cultural biography of things: Commoditization as process. In A. Appadurai (Ed.), *The social life of things: Commodities in cultural perspective* (pp. 64–91). Cambridge: Cambridge University Press.

Korf, B., Engeler, M., and Hagmann, T. (2010). The geography of warscape. *Third World Quarterly, 31*(3), 385–399.

Kornberger, M., and Carter, C. (2010). Manufacturing competition: How accounting practices shape strategy making in cities. *Accounting, Auditing, and Accountability Journal, 23*(3), 325–349.

Lefebvre, H. (1992). *The production of space.* Oxford: Wiley-Blackwell.

Leibold, A. M. (2011). Aligning incentives for development: The World Bank and the Chad-Cameroon oil pipeline. *Yale Journal of International Law, 36,* 167–205.

Lemke, T. (2001). The birth of bio-politics: Michel Foucault's lecture at the Collège de France on neo-liberal governmentality. *Economy and Society, 30,* 190–207.

Li, F. (2009). Documenting accountability: Environmental impact assessment in a Peruvian mining project. *Political and Legal Anthropology Review, 32*(2), 218–236.

Li, F. (2011). Engineering responsibility: Environmental mitigation and the limits of commensuration in a Chilean mining project. *Focaal: Journal of Global and Historical Anthropology, 60,* 61–73.

Li, F. (2015). *Unearthing conflict: Corporate mining, activism, and expertise in Peru.* Durham: Duke University Press.

Magnant, J. P. (1986). *Terre Sara terre Tchadienne.* Paris: L'Harmattan.

Magrin, G. (2001). *Le sud du Tchad en mutation des champs de coton aux sirènes de l'or noir.* Montpellier: Centre de Coopération Internationale en Recherche Agronomique pour le Développement.

Mallaby, S. (2004). *The world's banker: A story of failed states, financial crises, and the wealth and poverty of nations.* New York: Penguin.

Massey, D. (1994). *Space, place, and gender.* Minneapolis: University of Minnesota Press.

Massey, D. (2005). *For space.* London: Sage.

Massumi, B. (1995). The autonomy of affect. *Cultural Critique, 31,* 83–109.

Mehta, L. (Ed.). (2009). *Displaced by development: Confronting marginalization and gender injustice.* New Delhi: Sage.

Miller, P. (2001). Governing by numbers: Why calculative practices matter. *Social Research, 68*(2), 379–396.

Modi, R. (Ed.). (2009). *Beyond relocation: The imperative of sustainable resettlement.* New Delhi: Sage.

Molé, N. J. (2010). Precarious subjects: Anticipating neoliberalism in Northern Italy's workplace. *American Anthropologist, 112*(1), 38–53.

Molyneux, M. (2008). The "neoliberal turn" and the new social policy in Latin America: How neoliberal, how new? *Development and Change, 39*(5), 775–797.

National Public Radio (NPR). (2001, April 11). Commentary: New trend for business endeavors with developing countries.

Navaro-Yashin, Y. (2007). Make-believe papers, legal forms and the counterfeit: Affective interactions between documents and people in Britain and Cyprus. *Anthropological Theory, 7*(1), 79–98.

Njoh, A. J. (1998). The political economy of urban land reforms in a post-colonial state. *International Journal of Urban and Regional Research, 22*(3), 408–424.

Njoh, A. J. (2000). Continuity and change in Cameroonian land policy. *Planning Perspectives, 15,* 241–265.

Oliver-Smith, A. (Ed.). (2009). *Development and dispossession: The crisis of forced displacement and resettlement.* Santa Fe, NM: School for Advanced Research Press.

Park, S. (2010). The World Bank's global safeguard policy norm? In S. Park and A. Vetterlein (Eds.), *Owning development: Creating policy norms in the IMF and the World Bank* (pp. 181–203). Cambridge: Cambridge University Press.

Peck, J., and Theodore, N. (2010). Mobilizing policy: Models, methods, and mutations. *Geoforum, 41,* 169–174.

Pegg, S. (2006). Can policy intervention beat the resource curse? Evidence from the Chad-Cameroon Pipeline Project. *African Affairs, 105*(418), 1–25.

Pegg, S. (2009). Chronicle of a death foretold: The collapse of the Chad-Cameroon Pipeline Project. *African Affairs, 108*(431), 311–320.

Polgreen, L. (2008, September 10). World Bank ends effort to help Chad ease poverty. *New York Times.*

Polgreen, L., and Dugger, C. (2006, February 11). Chad's oil riches, meant for poor, are diverted. *New York Times.*

Poulantzas, N. (1972). *Pouvoir politique et classes sociales.* Paris: Maspero.

Reno, J. (2009). Your trash is someone's treasure: The politics of value at a Michigan landfill. *Journal of Material Culture, 14*(1), 29–46.

Reno, W. (2001). How sovereignty matters: International markets and the political economy of local politics in weak states. In T. M. Callaghy, R. Cassimir, and R. Latham (Eds.), *Intervention and transnationalism in Africa: Global-local networks of power* (pp. 197–215). New York: Cambridge University Press.

Richard, A., and Rudnyckyj, D. (2009). Economies of affect. *Journal of the Royal Anthropological Institute, 15,* 57–77.

Riles, A. (1998). Infinity within the brackets. *American Ethnologist, 25*(3), 378–398.

Robinson, R. (1972). Non-European foundations of European imperialism: Sketch for a theory of collaboration. In R. Owen and B. Sutcliffe (Eds.), *Studies in the theory of imperialism* (pp. 117–142). London: Longman.

Roitman, J. (2004). Productivity in the margins: The reconstitution of state power in the Chad basin. In V. Das and D. Poole (Eds.), *Anthropology in the margins of the state* (pp. 191–224). Santa Fe, NM: School of American Research.

Roitman, J. (2005). *Fiscal disobedience: An anthropology of economic regulation in Central Africa.* Princeton, NJ: Princeton University Press.

Ross, M. L. (1999). The political economy of the resource curse. *World Politics, 51*(2), 297–322.

Sachs, J. D., and Warner, A. M. (1995). *Natural resource abundance and economic growth.* NBER Working Paper no. 5398. Cambridge, MA: National Bureau of Economic Research.

Sawyer, S. (2004). *Crude chronicles: Indigenous politics, multinational oil and neoliberalism in Ecuador.* Durham, NC: Duke University Press.

Shamir, R. (2010). Capitalism, governance, and authority: The case of corporate social responsibility. *Annual Review of Law and Social Science, 6,* 531–553.

Shever, E. (2008). Neoliberal associations: Property, company, and family in the Argentine oil fields. *American Ethnologist, 35*(4), 701–716.

Shever, E. (2012). *Resources for reform: Oil and neoliberalism in Argentina.* Stanford, CA: Stanford University Press.

Shihata, I. (2000). *The World Bank in a changing world: Selected essays and lectures.* New York: Springer.

Shore, C., and Wright, S. (1997). Policy: A new field of anthropology. In C. Shore and S. Wright (Eds.), *Anthropology of policy: Critical perspectives on governance and power* (pp. 3–42). London: Routledge.

Shore, C., and Wright, S. (2011). Conceptualising policy: Technologies of governance and the politics of visibility. In C. Shore, S. Wright, and D. Pero (Eds.), *Policy worlds: Anthropology and the analysis of contemporary power* (pp. 1–25). New York: Berghahn Books.

Szablowski, D. (2002). Mining, displacement, and the World Bank: A case analysis of Compania Minera Antamina's operations in Peru. *Journal of Business Ethics, 39,* 247–273.

Tcheyan, N. O. (2003, October 10). Remarks by Nils O. Tcheyan, Director, Strategy and Operations, Africa Region Vice Presidency, World Bank-Komé. Accessed on-line at: http://www.essochad.com/Chad-English/PA/Newsroom/TD_Speech_101003_5 .aspx

Thompson, M. (1979). *Rubbish theory: The creation and destruction of value*. Oxford: Oxford University Press.

Thompson, V., and Adloff, R. (1960). *The emerging states of French Equatorial Africa*. Stanford, CA: Stanford University Press.

Trouillot, R. (2001). The anthropology of the state in the age of globalization: Close encounters of the deceptive kind. *Current Anthropology, 42*(1), 125–138.

Trouillot, R. (2003). *Global transformations: Anthropology and the modern world*. New York: Palgrave Macmillan.

Tuan, Y. F. (1990). *Topophilia: A study of environmental perception, attitudes and values*. New York: Columbia University Press.

United Nations Conference on Trade and Development. (2013). *World investment report 2013: Global value chains: Investment and trade for development*. New York and Geneva: United Nations.

Uriz, G. H. (2001). To lend or not to lend: Oil, human rights, and the World Bank's internal contradictions. *Harvard Human Rights Journal, 14*, 197–231.

Van der Ploeg, F. (2006, May). *Challenges and opportunities for resource rich economies*. CEPR Discussion Paper no. 5688. London: Center for Economic Policy Research.

Vogler, C. (2002). Social imaginary, ethics, and methodological individualism. *Public Culture, 14*(3), 625–627.

Watts, M. J. (2004a). Resource curse? Governmentality, oil and power in the Niger Delta, Nigeria. *Geopolitics, 9*(1), 50–80.

Watts, M. J. (2004b). Antinomies of community: Some thoughts on geography, resources and empire. *Transactions of the Institute of British Geographers, 29*(2), 195–216.

Watts, M. J. (2005). Righteous oil? Human rights, the oil complex and corporate social responsibility. *Annual Review of Environment and Resources, 30*, 373–407.

Weiner, A. B. (1992). *Inalienable possessions: The paradox of keeping while giving*. Berkeley: University of California Press.

Welker, M., Partridge, D. J., and Hardin, R. (2011). Corporate lives: New perspectives on the social life of the corporate form: An introduction. *Current Anthropology, 52*(S3), S3–S16.

World Bank. (n.d.-a). Chad: Poorest of the poor. Accessed on-line at: http://web .worldbank.org/archive/website01210/WEB/0__CO-48.HTM

World Bank. (n.d.-b). *The World Bank's approach to grievance redress in projects*. Washington, DC: Author.

World Bank. (1980, February 27). *Operational Manual Statement 2.33, social issues associated with involuntary resettlement in bank-financed projects*. Washington, DC: Author.

World Bank. (2000, June 6). World Bank approves support for Chad-Cameroon Petroleum Development and Pipeline Project. Retrieved from http://go.worldbank.org /HEIYT0LAT0

World Bank. (2001, February 21). World Bank appoints International Advisory Group on the Chad-Cameroon Petroleum Development and Pipeline Project. Press release no. 2001/235/S. Washington, DC: Author.

World Bank. (2004). *Involuntary resettlement sourcebook: Planning and implementation in development projects.* Washington, DC: Author.

World Bank. (2013). *Global review of grievance redress mechanisms in World Bank projects.* Washington, DC: Author.

Wroughton, L. (2007, March 22). World Bank tells Exxon to fix Chad compensation. Reuters.

Yergin, D. (1993). *The prize: The epic quest for oil, money and power.* New York: Free Press.

Yngvesson, B. (1976). Responses to grievance behavior: Extended cases in a fishing community. *American Ethnologist, 3*(2), 353–373.

Zalik, A. (2004). The Niger Delta: "Petro violence" and "partnership development." *Review of African Political Economy, 31*(101), 401–424.

INDEX

NOTE: Page numbers followed by *t* indicate a table.

LORI LEONARD is an associate professor in development sociology at Cornell University.

Lightning Source UK Ltd.
Milton Keynes UK
UKOW06f0210080616

275792UK00018B/114/P